The Worry Workbook for Kids

Helping Children to Overcome
Anxiety & the Fear of Uncertainty

MUNIYA S. KHANNA, PhD
DEBORAH ROTH LEDLEY, PhD

Instant Help Books
An Imprint of New Harbinger Publications, Inc.

Publisher's Note

Distributed in Canada by Raincoast Books

Copyright © 2018 by Muniya S. Khanna and Deborah Roth Ledley
        New Harbinger Publications, Inc.
        5674 Shattuck Avenue
        Oakland, CA 94609
        www.newharbinger.com

INSTANT HELP, the Clock Logo, and NEW HARBINGER are trademarks of New Harbinger Publications, Inc.

Cover image is a model for illustrative purposes only.

Cover design by Amy Shoup

Acquired by Tesilya Hanauer

Edited by Marisa Solis

Illustrations by Noah Grigni

Library of Congress Cataloging-in-Publication Data

Printed in the United States of America

23   22   21

10   9   8   7   6   5

To my parents, Shyamal and Ruby, for everything I have and ever will achieve—it is because of you.

To my husband, Vijay, for your undying passion, brilliance, and humor, and to Ishani and Sammy—you make it so easy to "create happiness."

—MK

To my mom, Roslyn Roth, for inspiring my interest in anxiety and worry; for encouraging me in everything I do; and for teaching me (through example) to be a wonderful mom.

To Gary, for always encouraging me professionally, while also being the best partner in parenting a girl could ask for.

And to Jenna and Matthew, for your helpful editing of this book and encouraging us to make it readable for all the kids out there!

—DRL

Contents

Breaking Out of the Worry Cycle
Step 3: Choose a Different Action

Breaking Out of the Worry Cycle
Step 4: Keep Practicing

Habits that Help

Foreword

Of all the challenges we face as parents, seeing our children wrestle with worry is one of the most difficult. Whether they are worrying about bees or homework, monsters under the bed or embarrassment in front of their friends, being away from home or even whether they are safe at school, children who worry are struggling with something that can feel out of reach to us and hard to fix: the products of their busy, fearful imaginations. We don't want our children to miss out on life, and at the same time, we ourselves are not sure how to convince them that they are okay when they are so convinced that they are not. As parents, we may be afraid that pushing kids into their discomfort zone will be too much for them.

Anxiety disorders in children are on the rise, with lifetime estimates as high as 24 percent. But the very good news is that children can learn so much about how to take charge of anxiety and buffer themselves from anxiety—with resilience under their wings rather than fear weighing on their shoulders. And parents are in the very best position to be the very best teachers. The wonderful book you hold now in your hands will help you lead the way.

Parents teach their children how to walk, tie their shoes, brush their teeth, look both ways before crossing the street—and the reason those lessons go so well is that parents know that their children need those skills in order be successful in life. So it is with anxiety management skills.

Fear is a normal and expected part of life; it rushes in and fills in the gaps between a child's learning about something new (like a dog) and learning how that experience really works (that dogs may be big and noisy but they are friendly, wonderful companions). Our instinct as parents is to protect our children from discomfort. We may want to whisk our children out of uncomfortable situations, having them skip activities like sports or school trips that may feel too hard. But here's the thing: being afraid of new situations isn't the problem, it's not even a sign of trouble, since most children feel that way.

The problem is when we inadvertently teach our kids that if/when they are afraid, they need to stay away in order to cope.

What is the alternative? We can teach our children a different response to fear: instead of trusting all the *what ifs?* and *oh nos!* that worry tells them, they can put these worries to the test and fact-check worry's story. Doing this fact-checking shrinks worry down to a much more manageable size. Then our children can be ready for the next step—approaching that fearful situation—which will seem much less daunting, even if it's one small step at a time.

One instinct we have as parents is to protect our children from suffering, but an equally strong instinct is to encourage and support our children's growth. Knowing how to handle fearful moments and shrink worry down to size doesn't always come naturally. It helps to have a guide. *The Worry Workbook*, written by my wonderful, gifted colleagues Drs. Muniya Khanna and Deborah Ledley at the Children's and Adult Center for OCD and Anxiety, shows parents and children how to use their smarts and not get taken in by the tricks worry can play. The step-by-step plan, complete with exercises and friendly illustrations, walks parents and children through worry moments and equips them with easy, effective strategies to understand how worry works, how to dismantle it, and how to prevail. More than just tackling the weeds of worry, *The Worry Workbook* provides exercises to plant the seeds of positive experiences such as creating happiness and cultivating gratitude—both of which buffer us from fear and contribute to a satisfying life.

It is never too early or too late to work on these skills with your children. *The Worry Workbook* has translated the most effective, empirically sound approaches to overcoming fear and anxiety into fun, accessible activities to work on with your child. And it is so much more than that. *The Worry Workbook* is a game changer, preparing children to be ready to take charge of the full range of life experiences they may face. It will be the beginning of a new sense of confidence for your child—for now and for a lifetime. Here's to less worry all around!

—Tamar E. Chansky, Ph.D.
Author of *Freeing Your Child from Anxiety: Practical Strategies to Overcome Fears, Worries, and Phobias*

Hello, Parents

If you picked up this book, it is probably because your child seems more stressed and anxious than he or she needs to be. No parent wants to see a child suffer, and we applaud you for seeking help. Your instincts are correct: There are simple changes in how your child approaches anxiety that can absolutely lessen how stressed and worried he or she feels.

We think you picked up the right book! This workbook is full of simple strategies based on decades of research that are designed to help children who struggle with anxiety, fear, and worry.

Children who struggle with worry have a near constant need for predictability, perfection, and planning. Why? All of these needs are aimed at avoiding "discomfort." It is totally normal for humans to want to avoid feeling bad, but sometimes this instinct becomes overactive and interfering. Our brains become focused on all the bad things that are happening or could happen in a situation, and we begin planning ways to "fix" it, prevent it from happening, or avoid it completely. After a while, our bodies and minds learn, incorrectly, that we can't handle discomfort and that we actually *are* in danger. Ironically, all the planning, prevention, and avoidance of bad things serve only to increase stress and anxiety. At its worst, it stops us from having fun, experiencing freedom, and enjoying important and meaningful life experiences.

Your child may worry mostly about his or her friendships, or mostly about grades and performance. Or she or he may worry all the time about everything (*What if I get in trouble? What if I fail? What if I'm late? What if I forget? What if they laugh?*). This book will be helpful for any and all of these types of worry, because all worry works in roughly the same way, and we fight it the same way no matter the content.

There are a lot of books on the market that tell parents how to talk to their child about anxiety. However, one frustrating hurdle is the firm resistance children have to listening to or considering another perspective. This workbook takes an action-based approach. In other words, we won't be lecturing your child in this book, and we're not encouraging you to either. Rather, your child will be learning by *doing*—she or he will be prompted to try lots of exercises and to practice them often.

Our approach includes self-talk and cognitive awareness training, along with experiential learning activities, that create opportunities to build mastery and create change. The behavioral practices are designed to bring new ways of thinking about and approaching uncertainty that will lead to lasting improvements in your child's ability to handle life's challenges.

We share *active* learning techniques in this workbook because they have been proven more effective than learning through reading, writing, or listening alone. We are appealing to the action-oriented parent and child, since this workbook is based on the principle that *doing* gives rise to *confidence*, rather than the other way around.

Keep in mind that you'll be serving as a "coach" or guide rather than as a parent or caretaker for the activities. The difference is that coaches set no expectation of how fast or how well a skill is to be learned; their job is to just facilitate practice. So while, as a parent, you will undoubtedly have the urge to set performance expectations, try to curb that in your new role as coach.

Our workbook is divided into three parts:

Understanding Worry, which describes the nature and symptoms of worry, and features exercises to foster knowledge

Breaking the Worry Cycle, a four-step guide on how to end the cycle of worry

Habits that Help, activities that support long-term benefit

Finally, we have included a "Tips for Parents" section on the website for this book (http://www.newharbinger.com/39638) that supplements the activities in this book. These tips give background and the rationale for concepts discussed. They'll also assist you in helping your child with follow-through. For maximum benefits, read the online tips before your child begins the work. You can also visit our website http://www.worrywisekids.org for even more tips and up-to-date research on anxiety and how to deal with it.

We hope that the skills we teach in this book will help your child embrace uncertainty—which will bring adventure, fun, and freedom back into his or her life. Let's get started!

Hi, Kids!

Are you feeling more stressed and nervous than you'd like?

If you are, then we're so glad you picked up this workbook! It's full of short and easy activities that will help you feel better and less stressed.

Anxiety (the feeling you have when you are worried or scared or nervous) stops you from doing fun and important things that you want to do (like making friends, getting your homework done, or trying out for a team). Worrying starts out seeming like you're just "planning" for tomorrow, but then it quickly becomes exhausting and stressful.

If fear and worry are holding you back, there is a lot you can do! You have taken the first step already by reading this page.

Your next step will be to try to do one or two activities from this workbook each week. You'll see how the activities help you "train" your mind and body to be better at letting worries go and to feel more confident when there may be some uncertainty or something new coming up.

By the end, you'll have a lot of tools in your pocket to use whenever you need, and you'll know enough to make you a real expert in getting through all kinds of scary situations.

You are on your way to having more fun and freedom! Good luck!

Understanding Worry

Why Do We Worry?

For You to Know

Your body has a built-in alarm known as the "fight-or-flight system." It's supposed to protect you in the face of danger (like if you were being chased by a bear). It's called "fight-or-flight" because the system gets your body ready to fight (punch the bear in the nose) or flee (run as fast as you can away from the bear).

Have you ever started to cross a street when all of a sudden you jumped back because you heard a car coming really fast? That was your body's alarm system protecting you by making you run back to the curb so you wouldn't get hurt.

But sometimes the alarm goes off even when you're not in danger. And sometimes it can happen at the weirdest times. For example, maybe you were just sitting at your desk getting ready to take a spelling test when suddenly your body felt as if it were being chased by a bear. Your alarm made you feel like things were not okay. You started to worry about all the bad things that could happen: *What if I fail? What if I forget all the spelling words?*

Do you notice that your alarm goes off more than it needs to? Does it seem like you've been feeling nervous or worrying more than you would like?

For You to Do

The first step in worrying less (or teaching your body that there's no bear behind you) is to know what your body feels like when the alarm goes off.

What happens in your body when:

- You hear a noise in the middle of the night?

- You see a scary part in a movie?

- Your teacher asks you to answer a question out loud in class?

- You have to perform in a recital, play in a big game, or take part in a competition in an hour?

When you're scared, how does your heart feel? Does it beat faster? What about your breathing?

Circle all of the things that you feel in your body when you are nervous or scared:

Fast heartbeat

Pounding heart

Blushing

Dizziness

Fast breathing

Shortness of breath

Butterflies in the tummy, feeling like you might throw up, or stomachache

Trembling or shakiness

Sweating or feeling warm

Needing to run and find a trusted person

Difficulty concentrating

Chills

These physical reactions (or feelings in your body) are all part of your body's alarm system. The alarm makes your heart beat fast and your breathing go faster to get air and blood to your muscles—so you can *run*! But look around. There's no bear.

Your body thinks you're in a dangerous situation. But you're not in danger. If you can remember that your body is just reacting to something it *thinks* is dangerous but is actually just new or uncomfortable, then you won't have to worry about the alarm as much.

More to Do

During the next few days, pay attention to your body's alarm system. Write down when your alarm goes off. Then describe how it makes your body feel.

Let's see if we can find any patterns.

Example:

My alarm went off when: I was getting ready to start at a new camp the next day and I was thinking that I might not make any friends.

My body felt: shaky, and I had butterflies. I felt like I wanted to be close to my mom.

1. **My alarm went off when** _____

_____

My body felt _____

_____

2.   **My alarm went off when** _____

_____

My body felt _____

_____

3.   **My alarm went off when** _____

_____

My body felt _____

_____

Aha! These are clues for when your alarm is likely to go off again. Next time you are in one of these situations, the alarm signals are likely to be back.

Can You Find Any Patterns?

A pattern is something that repeats itself in the same way over and over again. It's helpful to spot patterns, because then you know what to expect.

Looking back at your list from the last few days, do you see any patterns for when your alarm goes off?

My alarm usually goes off when:

1. _____

_____

2. _____

_____

3. _____

_____

These are the situations when your body shows you that you're nervous or that you're worrying too much. Your body's alarm will be in the habit of going off again in the same types of situations.

It's helpful to spot your alarm pattern because then you won't feel as surprised or worried the next time it comes up. It also gives you a chance to change something if you don't like the pattern you are in.

The Worry Cycle

For You to Know

When you are about to do something new, difficult, or uncomfortable (like presenting a book report to your class, inviting someone to your house for the first time, or going somewhere new without your mom or dad), your alarm goes off. Your body reacts as if it's in danger. Your mind starts thinking about all the bad things that could happen. Guess what? You're caught in a Worry Cycle.

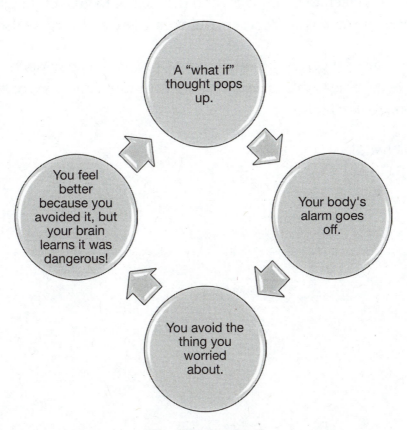

A "what if" thought pops up.

Your body's alarm goes off.

You avoid the thing you worried about.

You feel better because you avoided it, but your brain learns it was dangerous!

The Worry Cycle

When you listen to your alarm system and avoid new and difficult situations, you are being tricked into believing two false things:

1. The situation really *is* dangerous!

2. You can't handle new, difficult, or uncomfortable situations.

If your brain tells you these two things over and over again each time you're faced with something scary, you're probably stuck in a Worry Cycle.

Let's see the Worry Cycle in action. Pretend that you get invited to a sleepover. You want to go but your alarm goes off. You're worried that you won't be able to fall asleep there. So you listen to your alarm and decide not to go. You might feel better in that moment because of your decision, but your body learns two false things:

1. Sleepovers are dangerous (in other words, bad stuff can happen at sleepovers like not being able to fall asleep, missing your mom and dad, or being scared in someone else's house).

2. You can't handle sleepovers.

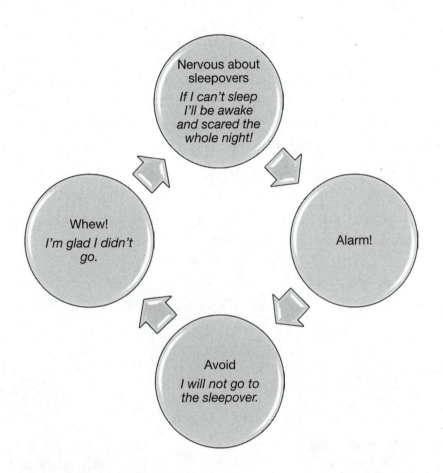

You're stuck in a Worry Cycle. Because now, *every time* you get invited to a sleepover, your alarm will go off, you'll worry, and you'll probably decide not to go.

But the truth is, the situation isn't dangerous—it just caused you to feel a little uncomfortable.

You *can* handle new, difficult, and uncomfortable situations.

For You to Do

To break *out* of the Worry Cycle, the first step is to figure out what is *in* the cycle. Fill in the blanks with a Worry Cycle you get stuck in sometimes. For more than one worry, you can use the My Worry Cycle worksheet at the back of this book, or draw your own cycle on a blank sheet of paper. Figuring out all the parts of your cycle helps you plan how to break out of it.

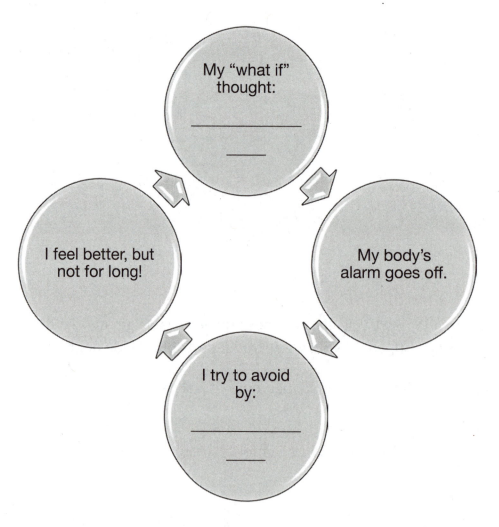

My Worry Cycle

The Worry Workbook for Kids

More to Do

Many times, kids or their parents will create a back-up plan or have a "safety net" in place when they have to do something that they may feel is dangerous. Here are three examples:

Sarah worries when her parents go out to dinner and leave her with a sitter. She always asks her mom to make sure she has her phone with her so Sarah can call her if she needs her. The phone becomes a *safety net* just in case Sarah needs anything from her mom.

Michael worries that he won't have fun if he doesn't know anyone at the party, so he calls his friend to make sure he is going. The friend becomes Michael's *safety net* just in case he doesn't know anyone else at the party.

Keisha felt dizzy at soccer practice one day. Ever since then, she worries that she might get sick if she does a lot of running around. Her mom tells her that she will stay at practice from now on (even though she used to drop her off) so that if Keisha feels sick they can leave. Keisha's mom becomes a *safety net* in case Keisha gets dizzy.

The problem is that safety nets and back-up plans—whether put in place by you or your parents—teach your brain that you really *are* in a dangerous situation that you can't handle. A safety net strengthens the Worry Cycle, making it last longer. The situation stays hard for longer when you use a safety net.

Look back at the Worry Cycles you have identified. Are there any safety nets you've put in place? If you're having a hard time filling in the lines below, ask a parent or someone who knows you well for help.

Do I Use Any Safety Nets?

1. When I worry about _____

I make sure I _____ just in case.

2. When I worry about _____

I make sure I _____ just in case.

3. When I worry about _____

I make sure I _____ just in case.

Breaking Out of the Worry Cycle

> ## *For You to Know*
>
> When you use safety nets, you continue to believe that safe situations are dangerous and that you can't cope with them. But the more you try to make sure nothing bad happens, such as with a safety net, the more you worry. The more you worry, the more often your alarm will sound in the same situation. And then you're caught in a Worry Cycle!

So far you have discovered that when you listen to your alarm system and avoid or plan how to get out of new and difficult situations, your body learns two false things:

1. The situation really *is* dangerous!

2. You can't handle new, difficult, or uncomfortable situations.

That's why your alarm keeps going off when you're faced with the same situation. You're stuck in a Worry Cycle! Ready to get unstuck?

There are four steps to breaking out of a Worry Cycle:

Step 1. Spot the false alarm. As soon as you notice your alarm has gone off, remind your body that the situation is not dangerous, just uncomfortable or difficult.

Step 2. Choose a useful thought. Challenge the worry and refocus your thinking. Remember that you have handled lots of new and difficult challenges.

Step 3. Choose a different action. Do the thing that worry tells you to avoid (without safety nets), and choose an action that will get you closer to your goal.

Step 4. Keep practicing. Repeat as often as possible in all kinds of situations!

The next sections of this workbook will help you get through these steps. Before you get started, let's plan which Worry Cycles you want to break out of.

For You to Do

We want to teach your body to recognize when you are not in danger, and that you *can* handle new, difficult, and uncomfortable situations. Let's make a plan to target the situations where you find yourself stuck in a Worry Cycle most often.

What are the worries or situations in which your alarm usually goes off? What are the new, difficult, or uncomfortable situations that you want to worry less about? Check off items on this list and then write down your own. Ask a parent or grown-up who knows you well for help, if you need it.

☐ *Inviting someone to get together*

☐ *Going to a new lesson or practice for the first time*

☐ *Working on a really important essay or project*

☐ *Having to face a fear (such as spiders, flying on an airplane, speaking to adults)*

☐ *Staying overnight at a new friend's house*

☐ *Doing something that you're not that good at*

☐ *Staying in one part of the house when everyone else is in another part*

☐ *Going to a place where you don't know anyone*

☐ *Doing a presentation in front of the class*

☐ *Participating in a new after-school activity*

☐ *Going to sleep without a parent or family member tucking you in*

☐ _____

☐ _____

☐ _____

☐ _____

☐ _____

☐ _____

More to Do

Now list three times when you handled a new, difficult, or uncomfortable situation. Describe the situation and then write down what you did. You can ask your parent or other grown-up who knows you well for help if you can't think of any.

Hint: *Have you ever started a new school year with a new teacher? Gone to a doctor's office that you were nervous about? Jumped into a pool even if you weren't that great at swimming? Played with someone you had never played with before at the park? Gotten lost but then found your way back to your parent or grown-up? Lost something you needed but then figured out how to replace it or be okay without it?*

Example:

The situation: Learning to ride my bike. I was very afraid of falling and hurting myself and having to go to the doctor.

It was new, difficult, or uncomfortable, but I was able to: finally ride without any help. I fell a bunch of times but I never had to see a doctor. They were just scratches and they healed.

1. **The situation:** _____

_____

It was new, difficult, or uncomfortable, but I was able to: _____

_____

_____

The Worry Workbook for Kids

2.   **The situation:** _____

_____

It was new, difficult, or uncomfortable, but I was able to: _____

_____

_____

3.   **The situation:** _____

_____

It was new, difficult, or uncomfortable, but I was able to: _____

_____

_____

See, you've handled lots of new and challenging things before! Most of the time they turned out not as bad as you thought. There were even times when trying something new was pretty great, right?

Breaking Out of the Worry Cycle

Step 1: Spot the False Alarm

Why Does My Tummy Hurt?

For You to Know

If a bear were chasing you, would it be a good idea to stop for lunch? No way! As part of your fight-or-flight response, your body shuts off your digestive system so it can concentrate on running.

Tummy aches come sometimes if you've eaten too much, or if you have a stomach bug, or even from doing too many cartwheels! But does your stomach ever feel "funny" or upset when you're worried or nervous? Have you ever felt "butterflies" in your tummy when you're in a new or scary situation, or before you have to do something you're uncomfortable with?

If so, you're not alone. All of us experience butterflies in our stomachs from time to time. That's because, as you learned in activity 1, when you're worried or feeling nervous, your body's alarm goes off. The fight-or-flight system starts your heart beating fast and quickens your breathing to get air and blood to your muscles—so you can *run*! Your body can't waste any energy on silly things like digesting your last meal!

When you are feeling worried or nervous, your stomachache is just part of a false alarm. Your body will turn off the alarm soon, and your tummy will feel better in no time. The achy feeling will come, and then it will go.

You don't need to do anything to make the butterflies go away—they will go away on their own. In fact, the very best thing do is to *keep doing what you were planning on doing* before your tummy started hurting. Before you know it, your stomach will feel much better.

For You to Do

Make a list of the times in the last few weeks when your alarm went off. These could be the same situations you wrote about in activity 1, or they could be new. Then write down whether you think it was a real danger or just a new, difficult, or uncomfortable situation. Write what ended up happening. What did you learn?

Example:

My alarm went off when: The night before I was leaving for sleep-away camp and I was thinking that I might be very homesick.

My body felt: shaky, and I had butterflies in my stomach. I felt like I wanted to stay home instead of go to camp.

Was this real danger? Or was it something new, difficult, or uncomfortable?

Real Danger   New, Difficult, or Uncomfortable

What ended up happening: I was a little homesick the first night, but once I settled in, I had so much fun!

1.   **My alarm went off when:** _____

_____

My body felt: _____

_____

The situation was: Real Danger   New, Difficult, or Uncomfortable

What ended up happening: _____

_____

2.   **My alarm went off when:** _____

_____

My body felt: _____

_____

The situation was: Real Danger   New, Difficult, or Uncomfortable

What ended up happening: _____

_____

3. **My alarm went off when:** _____

_____

My body felt: _____

_____

The situation was: Real Danger   New, Difficult, or Uncomfortable

What ended up happening: _____

_____

Next time you're in similar situations, remember that your body's alarm may have gone off, but it's just a false alarm. Your body thinks you're in danger, but it's just a new or difficult situation.

More to Do

In the coming week, write down all the times when your tummy hurts because you were worried or nervous. (Before school? During a math quiz? Before a piano lesson that you didn't feel quite ready for? On the way to a birthday party? When you didn't know what the plan was for the day ahead?)

My tummy hurt when _____

_____

My tummy hurt when _____

_____

My tummy hurt when _____

_____

My tummy hurt when _____

_____

My tummy hurt when _____

_____

These are clues for when the butterflies are likely to appear again. Remember, your body's alarm is in the habit of going off in the same types of situations. Next time you are in one of these situations, the butterflies are likely to be back.

Your alarm will tell you, "Don't do it! You're not okay! Lie down instead!" That's the time to remind your body that it's just sounding a false alarm. Say to yourself, "I'm not in danger, I'm just worried. My tummy will feel better soon." Then keep doing whatever you were doing before the feeling came.

Worry Is Like a Bully

For You to Know

Because worries can keep you from doing what you really need or want to do, it can be helpful to think of them as bullies. And just like with real-life bullies, if you take control away from worries by not giving them your time or attention, they will lose their strength and leave you alone.

Think of a bully bothering a boy at lunch. A bully might say, "Give me your lunch money or I'll beat you up!" If the boy gives up his lunch money, the bully might leave him alone that day, but chances are he will be back again tomorrow—because he got what he wanted. Every time he comes and gets what he wants, the bully gets stronger, more confident, and harder to ignore.

Worries are just like a bully: they tell you that bad things are out there or that bad things are going to happen so that you'll pay attention and do what they tell you. They may have started out trying to protect you (your alarm system kicked in), but after a while, they like that you listen to them so much that they keep telling you about more bad things that can happen. After a while, worries are not really protecting you anymore. They've become so *overprotective* that now they're more like a bully, trying to control you and stop you from doing what you want. The more you listen to them, the more often they come and the stronger they get!

But what if the boy doesn't give the bully the lunch money? What would probably happen next? The bully might try even harder with more threats. But if the boy *still* ignored the bully, walked away, found another friend and started playing something else (and we'd want him to tell a grown-up too), and didn't give the bully the money, the bully would see that he's not going to get what he wants. Eventually the bully would probably get bored and leave the boy alone.

The Worry Workbook for Kids

It works the same with worries. If you stay firm, don't give them your attention, and don't let them stop you from what you want to do, they lose strength and eventually leave you alone.

For You to Do

You can get faster at ignoring worry if you can identify the things that you are hearing from the "bully" or the worry most often. Circle the worry statements that pop up for you.

Fill in the blanks with other things worry likes to say to you:

These are the things worry says to keep you from doing what you want to do. But don't believe them! Keep doing what *you* want to do and *take control* back.

More to Do

What has worry stopped you from trying? Make a list of things that you've been too worried to try:

1. _____

2. _____

3. _____

4. _____

These are the things worry keeps you from doing. But don't let your worries bully you! Do what *you* want to do, and don't give the worries your time or attention.

Activity 6 — Let It Come and Go

When your alarm goes off, it is completely normal for your body to take a little while to return to normal and for all those emergency body reactions, such as a racing heart or a tummy ache, to go away. In other words, you don't have to do anything to fix the reactions. Your internal reset button does that work for you.

Imagine you're at the top of a slide. You push yourself down the slide, but then halfway down you decide you want to turn around. What do you do? It would be easier to just go down to the bottom and then "restart," rather than try to stop midway and climb back up the slide. Because once you start going, it's hard to reverse your course!

Just like letting yourself go down a slide, let your alarm signals run their course. It is much harder to try to suddenly force worries to stop or to make your butterflies go away. It takes a few minutes for your body to reset back to normal, but it will.

For You to Do

Have you ever tried to make uncomfortable body reactions or anxious feelings go away by taking a nap, calling mom or dad, going to the nurse's office, or staying home instead of going somewhere you were supposed to go? You might have found that the feeling ended up lasting a long time or got even worse than the last time you were in a similar situation. That's because when you try to make the feeling go away, your body learns that the feelings must be dangerous—so the alarm keeps going.

To make your anxious feelings calm down or go away, it's better not to focus on the feelings. They will go away on their own in a few minutes if you don't pay too much attention to them.

List the ways you may have tried to "make" worries or anxious feelings go away (for example, staying close to mom or dad, avoiding certain foods, avoiding certain activities, and so on):

I have tried to "make" my alarm signals go away by:

1. _____

_____

2. _____

_____

3. _____

_____

More to Do

Some kids worry when they notice an alarm signal. Just remember this: your body is like a noisy refrigerator.

Sit in your kitchen near the refrigerator for a few minutes during a time when there is no one in the room and it is quiet. Do you notice how noisy your refrigerator is? Refrigerators actually make a lot of racket all day long—there's spurting and revving and jingling—pretty noisy! But when you are in your kitchen and it's full of people, you don't realize that it's making any sounds at all.

Your body does the same thing. It's doing weird jingling and popping and wiggling all day long. But usually when we're around people or doing things that are active, we don't notice it.

If you start noticing all the little blurps and wiggles, you might get worried that something is wrong. Fear might even try to get your attention and make you think about bad things that could be happening…*Am I going to be sick? Do I have a weird disease? Is something wrong with me? Do I feel warm? Is my headache lasting longer than usual? Why do I feel a little dizzy?* And on…and on…

It's a trick! Don't give your alarm signals your time and attention. When you do, it makes the alarm ring even louder, you worry even more, and signals become stronger and last longer.

One of the best things you can do is take a few breaths (see activity 21), then go back to doing what you were doing as soon as you can. Let the feelings and noises come and go.

This week, practice letting the alarm signals come and go without trying to "make" them go away. Then list three times when you reminded yourself to ignore the "noisy refrigerator" and let the alarm come and go.

Example:

My alarm went off when: I was getting ready for baseball practice.

These were the alarm signals I noticed: I started to get hot and sweaty. I started having thoughts that I was going to strike out. I also started to pack my bag really slowly.

Instead of trying to "make" the feeling go away, I: Finished packing my bag and then played a video game until it was time to go.

1. **My alarm went off when:** _____

_____

These were the alarm signals I noticed: _____

_____

Instead of trying to "make" the feeling go away, I: _____

_____

2. **My alarm went off when:** _____

_____

These were the alarm signals I noticed: _____

_____

Instead of trying to "make" the feeling go away, I: _____

_____

3. **My alarm went off when:** _____

_____

These were the alarm signals I noticed:_____

_____

Instead of trying to "make" the feeling go away, I: _____

_____

Breaking Out of the Worry Cycle

Step 2: Choose a Useful Thought

Thinking About Your Thinking

For You to Know

You may not notice it, but in your mind, you say things to yourself all the time. These are your "thoughts." Some people call it your "inner voice," others call it your "self-talk."

In your mind, you constantly have thoughts about what you've learned, what you've decided, what you're planning, what you remember, what you think about different situations—all the time. It's really important to notice what you are thinking because your thoughts—the things you say to yourself—impact how you feel.

What I think → What I feel

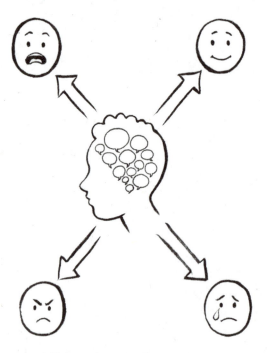

Thoughts → Feelings

In other words, your thoughts, or the things you are saying to yourself, can make you feel happy, excited, worried, angry, sad—all sorts of emotions. Let's try right now to listen to what your mind is saying.

Take a minute to close your eyes, and try to not focus on anything going on "outside" of your mind. Now try to listen to the conversation you are having in your mind. What are you thinking about right now?

Here are some questions that might help you "listen" to your thoughts:

What images or pictures do I see?

Am I thinking about something that is going to happen in the future?

Am I remembering something that just happened a few minutes ago? Or something that happened a few days ago?

Am I thinking about how someone might have thought of me (for example, thinking about what your teammates might have thought when you struck out at baseball)?

For You to Do

You may think that it's the situation that makes you feel a certain way, but it's really how you are *thinking* about the situation (your self-talk) that makes you feel the way you feel.

Need some convincing? Well, imagine that two kids are both in class when the teacher announces, "Surprise! We're going to an amusement park for a field trip next week!"

Though they are both in the same situation, the students have different thoughts about the teacher's surprise, and therefore they feel very differently.

	Situation	*Thought*	*Feeling*
Student 1	We're going to an amusement park!	I hate roller coasters. Everyone will go and tease me because I don't. I'll be the only one just waiting on the bench all day. I don't want to go!	Worried, sad
Student 2	We're going to an amusement park!	I love roller coasters! I can't wait to have cotton candy and a day of hanging out with friends!	Excited, happy

Can you now imagine situations in which you can feel good or bad depending on how you are thinking about it? Here are two situations to get you started.

See if you can guess what these kids are thinking that would make them feel the way they do:

	Situation	Thought	Feeling
Student 1	Next period is recess.		Worried
Student 2	Next period is recess.		Happy

	Situation	Thought	Feeling
Student 1	Camp starts next week.		Sad
Student 2	Camp starts next week.		Excited

More to Do

What you are thinking—the things that you are picturing and saying to yourself—are very powerful in affecting emotions, or how you feel.

Let's do a little experiment. Think about a time when you were on your favorite family vacation. Picture it. Remember your favorite thing about it.

How do these thoughts make you feel right now?

Now think about a different time, a time when something really bad happened, and it was really upsetting for you. Picture the worst part about it.

How do these thoughts make you feel right now?

Notice that just by thinking something different, you changed how you felt in just a few seconds.

Knowing what we are thinking or what we are saying to ourselves is very important, because how we think about things is very powerful in affecting how we feel.

Let's practice listening to our self-talk this week. It's a good time to pay attention when you notice your mood change—like from feeling okay to sad or happy to angry. Each day for the next few days, write down your self-talk (what you were thinking) during a time when you had strong feelings. What did you say to yourself?

When I was feeling WORRIED, I was thinking: _____

_____

When I was feeling HAPPY, I was thinking: _____

_____

When I was feeling ANGRY, I was thinking: _____

_____

When I was feeling SAD, I was thinking: _____

_____

Knowing what you're thinking will give you a lot more control over your worries and feelings, so keep practicing!

Turning Anxious Thoughts into Useful Thoughts

Worries are almost always thoughts about something bad happening in the future. They often start with the words "What if…"

What if I mess up and everyone makes fun of me?

What if I get sick in school? **What if** I throw up?

What if I miss my parents and I want to come home?

What if I get a bad grade and my parents get angry with me?

Anxious thoughts are usually about you believing that you can't do something. Anxious thoughts usually begin with "I can't," "I should," "I never," or "I always."

"**I can't** score any goals!"

"**I never** have fun because I don't play well!"

"**I should** work harder."

"**I always** do worse than all the other kids!"

Remember, don't let anyone, especially yourself, tell you things that aren't true!

Turning Anxious Thoughts into Useful Thoughts

Your goal is to become really good at making sure the thoughts you have are as *accurate* and *useful* as possible, and that they are not making you feel worse than you need to.

For You to Do

It can seem as if worries help us prepare or plan to make sure nothing bad happens, but, in reality, they take time away from what we really need or want to do. Worries tend to really mess things up!

List some of the "What if," "I can't, "I never," "I always," or "I should" thoughts that you notice most often in your self-talk:

1. _____

2. _____

3. _____

4. _____

5. _____

Keep in mind that we aren't saying you should think everything is great all the time. However, we want your thoughts to be accurate—not overpredicting or focusing on bad possibilities. If you can "challenge" your worries, you can ask yourself whether they are things you really need to worry about. And if you can be really quick to challenge your worries, they won't take time away from focusing on doing what you want or need to be doing.

Turning Anxious Thoughts into Useful Thoughts

Practice using these "challenge" questions whenever your alarm is going off or when one of your worries is popping up and interrupting your day (or night).

- My worry thought is telling me that the "worst thing ever" will happen. But what really is most likely to happen?

- What are *all* the things that could happen? The good things? Bad things?

- I've had this worry before—what usually happens?

- Just because I think it, doesn't mean it's true. Is this thought the most accurate or the most useful thought I could have in this situation?

- My worry thought always says that if this goes badly, my life will be ruined. But is this really a "life ruining" situation? Or just a tough situation?

- Worry likes to use old tricks to get me to pay attention. Is this a false alarm? Do I have to pay attention to this thought? What was I doing before this worry popped up?

- Is this useful to be thinking about right now? How much time do I want to spend thinking about it in this way?

- I can't control what ends up happening, but I can control what I choose to think, feel, and do. What do I want to do about this?

More to Do

See if you can use the challenge questions (or your own challenges) to turn the following worries into accurate and useful thoughts.

Friend Worries

My two friends are playing with each other and leaving me out. What if they don't like me as much as they like each other?

Challenge question that can help: _____

_____

What if I say the wrong thing and sound stupid in front of everyone?

Challenge question that can help: _____

_____

School Worries

What if I'm never going to be good at this? Everyone else gets it, but I don't.

Challenge question that can help: _____

_____

I'm so behind, I'll never finish! And I'll be in so much trouble tomorrow.

Challenge question that can help: _____

_____

Health Worries

My stomach hurts. I am sure I am going to throw up in school and embarrass myself.

Challenge question that can help: _____

_____

Mom says she has a headache. Maybe she really has a disease and is going to die.

Challenge question that can help: _____

_____

For You to Know

Your *focus*, or what you give your attention to, is a very important and powerful thing. What you focus on determines how you feel and what actions you choose to do next. So it's very important to choose your focus wisely. Whatever you focus on, what you spend the most time thinking about, is what your day becomes about.

If you focus on something bad that could happen in the future, or the bad things about a situation, you will feel worried, nervous, anxious, or sad. Likewise, if you focus on something you feel lucky to have or on something good that lies ahead, you will feel calm, happy, or even excited.

It's important to remember that *you* control the focus of your thoughts. You decide what your mind "zooms in" on, and that's how you can choose how you want to feel.

For You to Do

When you focus on negative and inaccurate thoughts or worries, you end up in a Worry Cycle. To avoid getting caught up in a Worry Cycle, challenge your thoughts and then focus on thoughts that are *accurate* and *useful*. When an anxious or worry thought pops into your head, try focusing on these useful thoughts instead. Here are some examples of helpful thoughts you can say to yourself instead of focusing on a worry:

- **This is temporary.** *It's not always going to be this way. Today is really hard, but tomorrow could be easier. The more I face these challenging things, the easier they will get. Things that seem very important today might seem really minor a week from now (and possibly even tomorrow).*

- **Don't stop trying.** *I can only learn from my experiences and keep getting better. There is no such thing as failure, just keep trying and get better each time.*

- **Little improvements make a big difference.** *I may not have won the race, but I beat my time from last week… I didn't get an A on my test but I understand this stuff better than I did before…*

- **Everyone makes mistakes.** *I can't expect to do everything perfectly. We're all human and we make mistakes. I will learn from my mistakes.*

- **I can choose my thoughts and feelings.** *I don't have to give time and attention to thoughts that are coming from worry. I can think about other things instead.*

- **I am in full control of my actions.** *Worry and sadness can't stop me from doing anything. I will continue to do what I want or need to do, even if it's uncomfortable or challenging.*

- **I will surround myself with positive people.** *There will always be people who say or think negative things about me. I can choose to stay focused on the people who bring positivity to my world.*

Let's practice focusing on more accurate and useful thoughts.

Use the Challenge Worry Worksheet to write down negative or worry thoughts you have been focusing on, then in the "Challenge the Worry" column, list other useful and helpful things you could think instead.

Fill in the situation, the thoughts, how they made you feel, challenges to the worry, and other things you could be focusing on that are more accurate and useful. If you have trouble with the last column, ask yourself, *What's most likely to really happen? What else is true? How useful is the thought? What do I choose to focus on?*

We've included an example so you can see how to use the worksheet.

Situation	Worry or Anxious Thought	Feeling	Challenge the Worry (think of a more accurate and useful thought)
Going to sleep	I'm going to have a nightmare. I'm not going to get enough sleep, and tomorrow I'll be really tired and have a bad day. What if someone breaks in?	Worried and anxious	I'm teaching my body that it's not in danger. This is just an uncomfortable thought. I'll let the alarm come and go. It's okay if I can't sleep. Eventually I will, and being a little tired is fine—that happens all the time and it's never a big deal. I know I'm safe. The worry is trying to get my attention. I'm lucky to have a comfortable home and family that loves me. Focus on what I want to do tomorrow.

Challenge Worry Worksheet

Situation	Worry or Anxious Thought	Feeling	Challenge the Worry (think of a more accurate and useful thought)

Keep practicing challenging worry by focusing instead on helpful things that make you feel calm or excited. You can use the blank Challenge Worry Worksheet at the end of this book to work through more worries.

More to Do

When focusing on what happened in the past, our brains tend to magnify the bad things and minimize the good things. We are more likely to remember something not so great rather than something really great.

What should we do instead? We should focus on the *present*—on what is happening right here, right now.

Susan worries a lot about school. She particularly worries about taking tests. Right now, Susan is studying for a math test that she has tomorrow at school. Let's take a peek inside her brain and see what she is focusing on:

Now that we have peeked inside Susan's brain, consider her thoughts. Write each thought in the correct column. Is it about the *past* (something that already happened); the *present* (what is happening right now); or the *future* (something that might happen at some later time)?

About the past	About the present	About the future

Is Susan focusing mostly on the past, present, or future?

_____

If you put all of Susan's thoughts in the past and future columns, you are spot on! Susan is supposed to be studying, but instead she is focusing on what happened during her last test, as well as what might happen on the next test.

What would be the most useful thing Susan could be focusing on *right now*?

Choose your focus wisely, because what you focus on decides how you feel and what actions you choose to do next.

Choose to Feel Good

For You to Know

When you worry, you start thinking about all the things you can't do and all the things you don't have. Don't let your worries "bully" you. Instead, try to focus your thoughts on the things you *can* do and all the things you *do* have.

Maybe you've thought, *I'm so tired of worrying!* Everyone feels this way at some point. There are times when it's okay to be bummed out. Sometimes things don't work out how we'd like, or they are harder than we'd expected them to be. But if you ever start to feel that you're spending too much time feeling sad and not enough time feeling relaxed and happy, try this: choose to feel good.

As you discovered in the previous activity, how you feel comes from your attitude, or how you're thinking about things. So if you choose to think about all the good things in your life, the people you love, the things you enjoy doing, or the good things in a situation, you will feel good.

When we focus on what we *don't* have, what we *can't* do, what *didn't* go well, or what *might* turn out badly, sad and worried feelings come. When we focus on what we *do* have, what we *can* do, and the times when things *do* go well, happy, content, and calm feelings come.

Let's look at the thoughts that created a worried and sad feeling for Mia.

Situation	Thought	Feeling
It's Wednesday and I'm at school.	I hate Wednesdays. It's not even close to the weekend. I still have to get through three long, boring, and hard days of school.	Worried and sad

But let's look at how Mia's attitude changed when she changed her thoughts:

Situation	Thought	Feeling
It's Wednesday and I'm at school.	Just two more days until the weekend. I did pretty well on my quiz. Maybe we can go see that movie on Saturday.	Good

We *can* choose how we want to think about the situation and how we want to feel. We *can* choose to feel good.

For You to Do

An important part of feeling happy and content in all sorts of situations involves remembering the things you *do* have. In every situation, you have a secret weapon: *you.* You are kind, helpful, funny, quick-thinking… You have people who love you and people who will always be there to help. Take a few minutes to list the things you *do* have:

List three qualities, strengths, or talents you are most proud of:

1. _____

2. _____

3. _____

List three people (pets can count too!) you love spending time with:

1. _____

2. _____

3. _____

List three things you enjoy doing:

1. _____

2. _____

3. _____

More to Do

In a situation this week when you are feeling down, practice choosing happiness. Focus on what you do have, what you do well, and what you can do to make the situation turn out as best as possible this time or next time.

I was thinking:

Situation	Thought	Feeling

Instead I thought:

Situation	Thought	Feeling

Activity 11

Having an Attitude of Gratitude

For You to Know

Gratitude is a big word that means "feeling thankful." Thanksgiving is one day each year when we think about all the things we are thankful for. But it's really good to think about the things we're thankful for every day. When we focus on the good things and on the things we're grateful for, we make our whole day better.

We often think about all the things we *don't* want (don't want to have a bad day, don't want homework), and all the things we want more of (more friends, more toys, more holidays). These thoughts make us feel worried, sad, and sometimes even angry.

If we fill our thoughts with what we don't have and what we don't want, we spend the day feeling worried, sad, and angry.

Sure, not every day can be great. We all have times when we feel left out, or we've been worrying about a big game or hard test, or something didn't go the way we had hoped. It isn't easy to feel good when your day feels tough.

But if you can pause and focus on the things you already have, the bad things become like little obstacles that you might notice but not need to give much time and energy to. When you're having a tough day, it helps to think of the things you're grateful for.

For You to Do

Take a few minutes to list the things you have that you are grateful for.

I Am Grateful For...

These people in my life:	
My hobbies and the things I like to do in my free time:	
Things in nature:	
Things I am good at:	
Songs, movies, and books that I love:	
Things that I've done or adventures I've had:	

My good qualities:	
Foods that I like to eat:	
A silver lining (something that seemed really tough but turned out to teach me something important):	

More to Do

Take a few minutes each day to write down the things you are grateful for. You can use the form we've included below. Or you can design your own form. Or you can be a bit freer with your format and start a "gratitude journal." This is a little notebook or journal where you can record on a daily basis the things you are grateful for. Feel free to keep your gratitude journal electronically (on your computer or in an app on your phone). However you record the things you are grateful for, it's a great way to start choosing what to focus on and what to fill your day with.

It's okay to repeat the same things on different days—that just means you're really lucky to have that great thing or person in your life! Eventually, try to think of new things to list, or try to focus on a different aspect of that person or thing.

Make it a habit to write down what you are grateful for daily (try right before bed or first thing in the morning). It just takes a couple of minutes. Don't think of it as a chore—consider it a time when you get to think about good stuff.

Where to start? Beyond what you've already listed in the "I Am Grateful For..." chart on the previous page, also consider:

- Things or people who make me laugh

- The people who love me

- My environment

- Experiences (interesting, fun, or learning adventures that I've had)

- Tastes and smells (yummy foods or items that always smell nice)

- Times people have been kind to me

- Things that I am proud of

- People or things that make my life easier or nicer

- People who help me, such as teachers, coaches, doctors, firefighters, and so on

- The "everyday" things that I might forget about (the car, bus, train, or plane that takes me where I need to go; grocery stores that have my favorite foods; traffic lights so people don't get stuck at corners; sports team that I like to watch and cheer for; my brain for making me so smart!)

The Things I am Grateful For

Date: _____

Three people I am grateful for:

    1. _____

    2. _____

    3. _____

Three things I'm grateful for:

    1. _____

    2. _____

    3. _____

Three nice things that happened today:

    1. _____

    2. _____

    3. _____

Breaking Out of the Worry Cycle

Step 3: Choose a Different Action

Doing New and Uncomfortable Things

For You to Know

The best way to do something you've never done before—
or do something that makes you uncomfortable—is to do
it gradually, a little bit at a time. When you can break down
a new or challenging thing into small steps, it won't feel as
overwhelming or scary. It's time to take action—*one step at a
time*!

We are now onto step 3 of how to break out of our Worry Cycles. Step 3 is all about
doing things differently.

So far in this workbook, you've been working on how to worry less by thinking
in a way that is accurate and useful in scary situations. How we *think* and *feel* in a
situation then impacts what we decide to *do* in the situation.

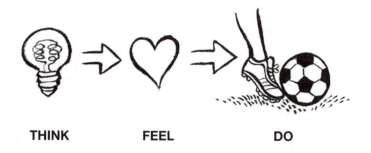

THINK   **FEEL**   **DO**

The Worry Workbook for Kids

The actions you choose are very important because they create the experiences you have today. These *experiences* shape what we think about ourselves and our world.

THINK   **FEEL**   **DO**

As you have learned, when a worry pops up and your alarm goes off, you usually start thinking of actions that will avoid or make sure the "bad thing" you're worrying about doesn't happen.

But then your *experience* ends up being that you *couldn't* handle it, and it really *was* dangerous. In order to teach your body that a new or uncomfortable situation is okay, you have to do the thing that you are avoiding. You have to show the worry that you can handle it (stand firm against the bully). And you can! "Doing the thing" means taking a small step toward doing what you have been avoiding—the thing the worry says not to do.

The good news is that if you choose to try doing the new or uncomfortable situation, or plan to take on the difficult situation instead of avoiding it, your body learns that the situation is *not* dangerous and that you *can* handle it. Only then does your alarm stop going off as often and the worries stop popping up and bothering you so much.

Activity 12　Doing New and Uncomfortable Things

We will be practicing trying new and uncomfortable things in this section. We will start with easy practices so you can build your strength and confidence until you're able to take on the most difficult challenges.

For You to Do

Jill, a sixth-grader, worried so much about school that she had not been to her classes for several weeks! Because tackling a worry this big at one time can be very hard, Jill found it much easier to break her worry into steps. She returned to school by first sitting in the main office in the mornings. After a few days, she went to just her first class. After that, she stayed for her second class. A few days later, she could stay at school all the way through lunch.

Taking things a step at a time worked great for Jill. At each step, she saw that the things she feared did not happen. And she realized that if there was a little challenge at school, like a tough test or a mean classmate, she could handle it. Seeing that she could handle one step increased her confidence about handling the next step. Before she knew it, Jill was back to spending the entire day at school.

In activity 3, you checked off several new, difficult, or uncomfortable situations that you want to worry about less. Then you added your own situations to the list.

Now pick one of those situations. Then, using the My Practice Ladder worksheet below, break it into five small, more-manageable steps. At the bottom of the ladder, put the easiest step. At the top of the ladder, put your hardest step. For each step, write down the days you will tackle these steps. This will keep you moving up your ladder to your ultimate goal! We have included Jill's practice ladder as an example.

Example:

The Worry Workbook for Kids

Jill's Practice Ladder: Worry About Going to School

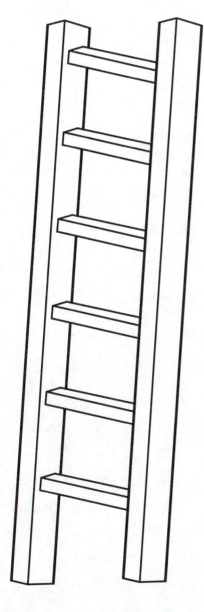

Step 5 (hardest): Stay at school for full day.

Days I will do this step: November 24, 28, 29

Step 4: Stay at school for morning class, lunch, and recess.

Days I will do this step: November 21, 22, 23

Step 3: Stay at school until lunchtime.

Days I will do this step: November 15, 16, 17

Step 2: Go to my first class.

Days I will do this step: November 10, 13, 14

Step 1 (easiest): Go into school and sit in main office for 20 minutes.

Days I will do this step: November 7, 8, 9

Helping Children to Overcome Anxiety and the Fear of Uncertainty

My Practice Ladder

Worry about _____

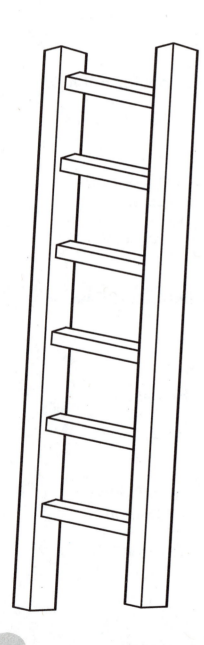

The Worry Workbook for Kids

More to Do

The Practice Ladder can be used for any worry. Think of other worries you want to tackle but that feel overwhelming. For each of these worries, build a ladder. Your ladder does not have to have five steps. If five steps seem overwhelming, make a longer ladder—you can make seven steps or even ten steps. You can find another blank copy of the My Practice Ladder worksheet at the back of this book.

Tackle one worry ladder at a time. Give yourself a few days at each step to get used to that experience, to see that nothing bad happens, and to show yourself that you can cope with whatever comes your way. Keep moving up your ladder to reach your ultimate goal!

And don't forget to reward yourself for a job well done. When Jill reached her goal of staying at school for the full day, her mom and dad took her out for her favorite pizza place for dinner!

Worry about _____

Choosing Actions

For You to Know

When we choose *not* to do something new or uncomfortable, we experience fear and worry. By avoiding that thing, we keep ourselves stuck in the fear and worry. How to get unstuck? We must choose to *do the thing*!

When you listen to your worries and try to avoid "bad things" from happening, you don't learn that:

1. The "bad thing" wasn't going to happen, and

2. Even if things don't turn out perfectly, you *can* handle it.

To teach yourself that things are okay, you have to do the thing you're afraid to do and prove that you can handle it. For example, if you have been avoiding sitting with other kids at lunch, you could plan to sit with another kid who may also be sitting alone. If you have been avoiding raising your hand in class, you could plan to raise your hand when there is a question that you know the answer to in your favorite class.

When trying to decide what to do instead when you're feeling worried or anxious, keep in mind these tips:

- Do the thing that you're afraid of.

- Do the *opposite* of what worry wants you do.

For You to Do

"Doing the thing," means taking a small step toward your end goal. Let's practice what "doing the thing" means. What would be an action that could lead these kids closer to their end goal?

1.   Luke wants to be a good swimmer, but he has been worried that he might not be able to pass the swim test. So he has been avoiding getting in the pool during his swim lessons.

Worry action: I sit on the bench during swim lessons.   →   **Experience:** I can't handle swim class, I'm not a good swimmer.

Do the thing: _____

2.   Vanessa wants to finish her homework, but she's worried that it's going to be really hard. So she decides to watch her favorite show first.

Worry action: I watch a TV show until I feel like getting started.   →   **Experience:** Homework is tiring and hard.

Do the thing: _____

More to Do

The actions that come from worry or fear are usually actions that avoid the situation or try to prevent anything bad from happening.

We recommend "doing the opposite" of what worry tells you. For example, if your worry says, "Don't raise your hand!", the opposite would be to raise your hand. If it says, "Don't touch that desk—that kid who was sick just touched it!", doing the opposite would be to touch the desk. If you are afraid to sleep alone at night, your worry would say, "Ask Mom or Dad to sleep with you," and doing the opposite would be to tell them to check on you after twenty minutes but not stay.

Take a look at one of your Worry Cycles. What does worry say you should do? This week, plan to practice "doing the opposite."

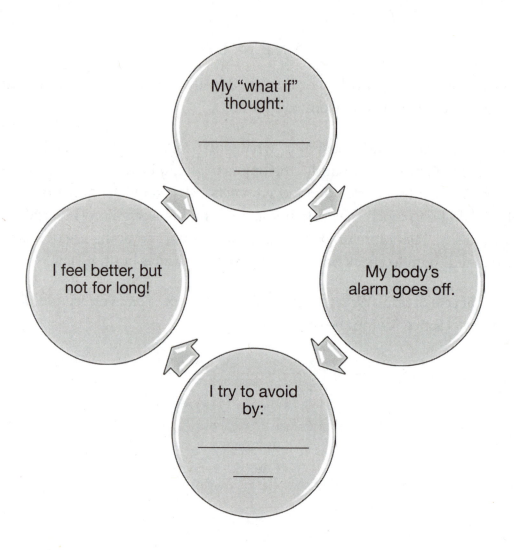

Worry action: _____

_____

The opposite: _____

_____

Getting Used to It

For You to Know

Our bodies have an incredible ability to adjust. They can get used to a new thing fairly quickly—as long as we're willing to be a little uncomfortable in the beginning. Remember the reset button you learned about in activity 6? In order to overcome a worry, you need to stay in the uncomfortable situation for long enough that your reset button clicks and your body starts to feel normal again. The more often your body can reset, the better chance your body has of getting used to the thing it used to be scared of.

One of the goals of the Practice Ladder is to give yourself a chance to get "used to" the difficult situations on your list. You might have to break it down into steps, but whatever you do, don't give up! The more you practice, the easier it will be to reach your goals.

Here's an example from Jasmine, who worries about going to houses with dogs. Jasmine has avoided dogs her whole life. She's avoided going to the homes of friends who have dogs, and she won't go to parks if she thinks dogs might be there. Jasmine tells her mom that she worries that dogs might bite her or jump on her. But when Jasmine begins to challenge her worry thought, she realizes that her worry is a false alarm.

Jasmine recognizes that many kids have dogs for pets, so they must not be that dangerous. In fact, she asked her friends about their dogs and learned that none had been bitten (beyond little puppy nibbles). She also learned that when dogs jump up on people, it is like a greeting. Jasmine found it quite helpful to focus on these accurate and useful thoughts instead of her worry thoughts. But, when it came to actually seeing a dog, Jasmine was still really afraid—even at her grandmother's house.

It's time to help Jasmine get "used to" dogs. It's time for a Practice Ladder.

Jasmine's Practice Ladder

Worry about: *dogs*

Sit in the same room with Grandmom, with her holding the dog on a leash, for 30 minutes.

Sit in the room next to the room with Grandmom and the dog for 30 minutes.

Go to Grandmom's house and ask Grandmom to keep the dog on a leash. Sit in the room next to the room with the dog in it for 20 minutes.

Go to a park where there might be some dogs. Stay for 15 minutes.

Walk down the street where a dog lives.

For You to Do

Getting "used to" something means having some patience. It might take several tries before you can reach your goal. Keep in mind that if you avoid the new or uncomfortable situation, your body will think the situation is dangerous. But if you can ride out the scary situation until the reset happens, your body will get used to the thing you used to be scared of!

Take one of your Practice Ladders and build in some time to get "used to" the situation that is difficult. You can add minutes or you can repeat one step a few times, as Jasmine did.

Worry about _____

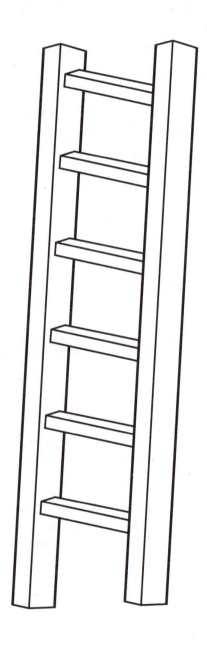

More to Do

If you were from a quiet town and you went to spend a few nights in a really loud city, you might have some trouble sleeping that night. You'd wonder how anybody could sleep with that noise! (The opposite might be true as well. If you were from a loud city and you went to spend a few nights in a very quiet town, you might have trouble sleeping too!)

That's because our bodies get used to our environment and our habits. Once we get used to something, it can be uncomfortable if it changes. If we worry about change and discomfort—and try to avoid it—we can get stuck in a Worry Cycle.

But remember that our bodies have an incredible ability to adjust. They can get used to a new environment or habit pretty quickly as long as we are willing to put up with some discomfort at first.

Away from your quiet town, you would eventually get used to sleeping in the noisy city—even thought it might mean a few nights of tossing and turning in the beginning. There's one exception, though: If your worry thought tells you, *I can't sleep, it's too loud!*, and you start watching TV all night, your body won't have a chance to get used to sleeping in that environment. Rather, it'll get used to watching TV at the time you should be sleeping!

But if you challenge your worry thought and choose a more useful and accurate thought like, *It's loud, but it's okay if I don't sleep as well as usual*, your body will learn that there's no need to sound the alarm. And each night you'd sleep a little better. Your body is really good at adjusting, as long as you let it.

Here are some ideas for "getting used to it" practices. If any of these things are difficult, or if you can think of anything else that has been difficult because you have avoided it for a long time, make a Practice Ladder and use your steps to help you get used to it again.

Practice 1: Teach your brain that the dark is okay

- Walk through a dark hallway on purpose.

- Go alone to a part of your house that you don't usually go to alone.

Practice 2: Teach your brain that foods that look unfamiliar are not dangerous

- Try a fruit you've never tried before.

- Try a food with a new sauce or made in a new way. For example, if you always have strawberry jam on your sandwich, try raspberry.

Practice 3: Teach your brain that new places and new people aren't dangerous

- Visit a park with your family that you've never been to before. Better yet, invite a new friend to come along!

- Next time your parents need to go out, be open to having a babysitter who has never stayed with you before.

Worry about _____

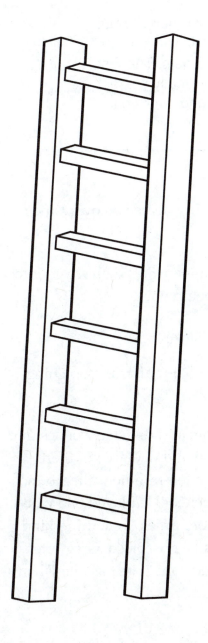

Activity 15 The More You Do It, the Easier It Gets

For You to Know

In order to get over the things that worry us, we need to put ourselves in scary situations. That's a hard thing to do. But here's the trick: the more you do it, the easier it gets. The first time we do a scary thing, we are likely to feel…really scared! But when we do that same scary thing over and over again, that scary feeling will eventually go away.

When we practice doing something scary, the anxious feeling decreases over time for a few reasons:

- We see that the things we were scared of did not happen. So, when we go into the situation the next time, we are less worried to begin with.

- We learn that we can cope with whatever comes our way.

- Our bodies learn that the situation isn't dangerous, so our alarms stop going off in that situation.

Let's meet Greg, who is scared of being away from his mom and dad. He worries that he can't handle something scary happening when his mom and dad are not there. The first time Greg's mom and dad left him alone (to take a ten-minute walk around the block), Greg was amazed to see that nothing bad happened. He played one video game and then they were home! After practicing many more times, something kind of scary did happen. When Greg's parents were out, he had a nosebleed. Greg often has nosebleeds, and he always worries about how he would cope if he has one when his parents are away. When his nosebleed started, he started to panic. But then he thought to himself, *I've handled nosebleeds tons of times*. With that thought, he calmed down, got some tissues, and, before he knew it, the bleeding stopped. Greg saw that he could cope all on his own.

Knowing that we can cope is an amazing confidence booster!

For You to Do

Pick a situation that makes you feel worried or scared. You can look back to activity 3 (Breaking Out of a Worry Cycle) for some ideas; choose one that you feel is just "a little difficult."

For the next week, go into that same situation every day. Try to keep the situation as similar as possible from day to day. When you finish your time in that situation, mark on the graph below how scared you felt using a 0 to 10 scale with 0 = not at all scared and 10 = extremely scared.

Here is a graph completed by eight-year-old Shawn, who avoids watching scary movies. This was starting to cause problems for Shawn because he didn't know what his friends were talking about at recess and lunch, and he avoided birthday parties that involved watching movies. Shawn didn't want to feel left out any more. So he made the choice to challenge his fears. Shawn decided to watch the first half hour of the same scary movie every day for a week to see what happened to his fear ratings.

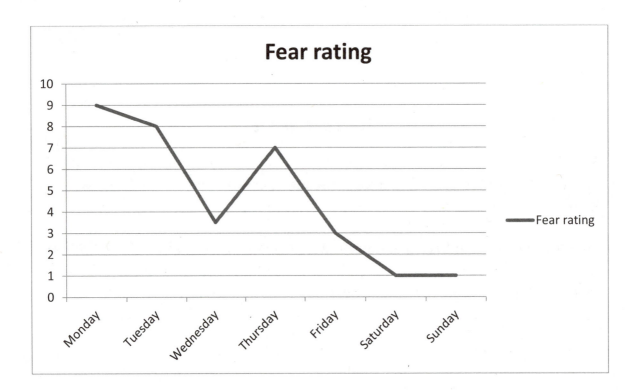

Below, you will find a blank graph to fill in during the coming week. To get started, first decide what feared situation you are going to work on and what your plan each day is going to be:

The More You Do It, the Easier It Gets   Activity 15

My feared situation: _____
_____

My plan: Each day, I will _____
_____

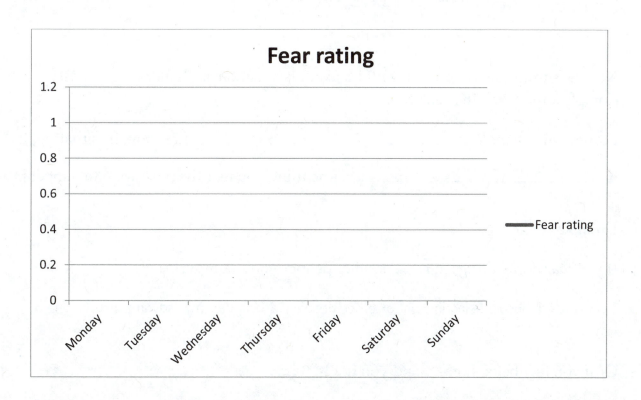

At the end of the week, connect your lines to form a line graph. What pattern did you observe at the end of the week?

_____

_____

_____

More to Do

Congratulations on practicing facing a situation that you considered "a little difficult"! Now, look back to activity 3 again and pick one of the situations that you consider would be "tough" to face but not "really hard."

Situation: _____

_____

Now let's think about how you could make this situation as challenging as possible. Complete the following sentence:

I could never handle _____ [the "tough" situation] if

if _____ [the thing you fear the most were to happen].

Example:

If you fear doing things in front of other people, you might write:

I could never handle being in front of other people if I dropped my tray in the lunch line at school.

Or if you fear being home alone, you might write:

I could never handle being home alone if there was a power failure.

Can you make this most feared situation happen? It will probably take a ton of bravery (like purposefully dropping your tray in the lunch line at school) and some advance planning (like having mom and dad switch off all the lights in the house before they leave you alone for ten minutes). But these kinds of experiences can teach us really powerful lessons.

After you have tried making the scary situation happen, answer the questions below:

Was the experience as bad as you predicted?

_____

_____

_____

Were you able to cope, even if you felt nervous or scared?

_____

_____

_____

What else did you learn?

_____

_____

_____

This exercise is likely going to cause you some anxiety. Repeat it in exactly the same way a few more times. Guess what? With repetition, even this scariest scenario will become quite a bit easier.

Activity 16 What You Can Control

For You to Know

What other people do or say is not in our control. And most things that happen to us aren't in our control either. We can't make anything happen exactly as we want or change what someone else thinks or does. But we *can* control how *we think* about a situation and what *we do* in that situation.

Bad things do happen sometimes. You might get a bad grade on your report card. Your best friend might move away. You may make a mistake on stage or mess up in a game. And you might feel sad, frustrated, maybe even angry. That makes sense! These feelings are normal reactions to disappointing situations.

However, your feelings can start to feel like too much when they prevent you from enjoying things you like to do. The bad thing doesn't have to stop everything else. It's time to take control of what you *can* control: how you *think* about this situation and what you choose to *do* next.

In every difficult situation, you can ask yourself: "What can I choose to think and do to make things turn out better?"

First, let's look at some examples of things that are *not* in your control:

If a friend is being mean, you can't change how he acts.

If your teacher is really strict, you can't make her more flexible.

If you work really hard on a project, you can't make your teacher give you a good grade for it.

But what *can* you control? How you *think* about the situation and what you *do* in the situation is in your control.

The Worry Workbook for Kids

For You to Do

What would you choose to do and think to make things turn out better?

To put this question to the test, let's say you try out for the baseball team and don't make it. Your worry—that you wouldn't make the team, where all your friends are—came true. You're disappointed that you've failed and that you won't be able to play with your friends after school. What can you control?

1. *Think* **about the situation in a way that is helpful.** Here are some things to remember:

   - It's temporary. Tell yourself, *Not making the team is a disappointment. But is it a* life-ruining *situation? Or is it just a tough one? Is it going to be a problem forever? Or just for a little while? If it were one of my friends who hadn't made the team, what would I tell him? What are all the things that could happen now? Are there good things as well as bad ones?*

   - You're human. No one is perfect. *Instead of deciding that you've failed, decide how you want to work on it more. Say to yourself, I'll work on my hitting and catching with my brother after school. I can play catch with my friends.*

   - Choose to focus on other things. Focus on things that are true and things that you have. Say to yourself, *I love baseball even when it's not baseball season. I can like baseball even when I'm not on the team. My friends and I play together all year long. I'm lucky I have friends who I like to play with, and I love playing baseball. I'm getting better every time I play.*

2. **Think about what you** *can do* **to make it a helpful experience.** Remember, worry will try to protect you by making you give up on baseball. But it won't really be protecting you. You'll be giving up something you love. You might even give up trying out for sports altogether, thinking you'll never be able to

succeed. Don't let worry sell you short! Try to do the things worry is telling you not to do. Here is what you might choose to do:

- Make some plans. *I can make a plan to play with my friends at the park.*

- Keep trying. *I can use the park games to work on my hitting and pitching. Then I can try out again next year—and maybe I'll make it!*

- Get help from others. *I'll ask my brother and my uncle to help me practice. I'll ask my mom if I can go to the park.*

- Try something different. *Maybe now I'll have time to try a new activity. I've always wondered what the school newspaper is like.*

Now let's practice with some problems that you might face. Practice using what you *can* control—how you choose to *think* and what you choose to *do*—to make things turn out better:

1. **Challenging situation:** *My parents are going out and I have to stay with a babysitter I don't know well.*

Choose my focus:_____

_____

Choose what to do: _____

_____

2.   Challenging situation: *I have so much homework that I won't have time to watch TV or do anything else.*

Choose my focus: _____

_____

Choose what to do: _____

_____

3.   Challenging situation: *I asked a friend to play and she said she was already playing with someone else.*

Choose my focus: _____

_____

Choose what to do: _____

_____

4.   Challenging situation: *I have basketball today and I forgot to wear sneakers.*

Choose my focus: _____

_____

Choose what to do: _____

_____

More to Do

From now on, when you face a challenge, use what you *can* control to make it better. This week, write down the different challenging situations that came up, as well as what you chose to *think* about and what you chose to *do*.

1. **Challenging situation:** _____

   _____

   I focused on: _____

   _____

   I chose to do: _____

2. **Challenging situation:** _____

   _____

   I focused on: _____

   _____

   I chose to do: _____

Create Happiness

For You to Know

Happiness is the feeling we get when we choose to *think* about all things we love and are grateful for. It also comes when we choose to *do* the things we enjoy doing. We can *create* our own happiness by doing things we are passionate about: the things we think are really fun, things we want to get better at, or things we think are important.

When we accomplish our goals, we feel happy. When we try something new that we've wanted to try, we feel happy. When we do something that helps others, we feel happy. Happiness is what happens when we do something that we love to do!

We all have different opinions about the things that bring happiness, because happiness has a lot to do with what we as individuals like to do—and that might be different from what our friends like to do. For example, some people are happy when they're fishing, while others find fishing to be boring. So what are your interests? What makes you smile? What makes you feel good?

There are some things that make you feel good right away but only for a short time (like eating ice cream or watching a TV show). Then there are things that might not feel great right away but make you feel good for a long time (like working really hard on making your own comic book and then, maybe after a few months, finally finishing it—and getting good at drawing in the process!).

Waiting for Happiness

Creating Happiness

The Worry Workbook for Kids

For You to Do

A great way to create happiness is to pursue a goal or an experience, like being able to play a full song on an instrument. Remember, set simple and realistic goals, ones that are challenging and exciting but not impossible or unlikely for you to achieve. Think of goals that you can reach in a few simple steps in the next few weeks.

List three things you want to get better at:

1. _____

2. _____

3. _____

Make plans for three things you can do this week toward your goal:

1. _____

2. _____

3. _____

List one little thing you can do today toward your goal:

1. _____

Think of the times when you feel most happy or most at peace. What are you doing? Make a plan right now to do that more often.

List three things you'd like to do more often.

1. _____

2. _____

3. _____

Make plans for three things you can do this week to do more of what you love:

1. _____

2. _____

3. _____

List one little thing you can do today toward doing more of what you love:

1. _____

More to Do

When we plan to bring joy to others, or do something that makes someone else laugh or feel good, we create happiness for them *and* for ourselves.

List three people you love and something you love about them (don't forget your pets!).

1. _____   1. _____

2. _____   2. _____

3. _____   3. _____

List three little things you can do that will make someone else happy today:

1. _____

2. _____

3. _____

Breaking Out of the Worry Cycle

Step 4: Keep Practicing

Sitting with Discomfort

For You to Know

Kids who worry tend to not only avoid new and uncomfortable situations, they also try to avoid new and uncomfortable sensations (like itchiness, tightness, or feeling warm, wet, or sticky). The problem is the same: the more they avoid these sensations, the more uncomfortable they feel. The trick is to help our bodies feel more comfortable by getting "comfortable being uncomfortable."

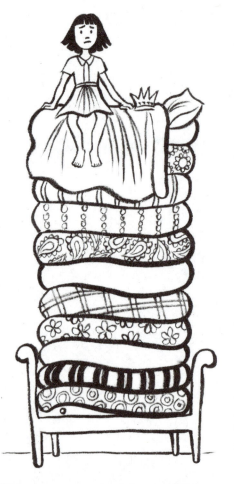

Have you heard the story "The Princess and the Pea"? In this fairy tale, the princess is so sensitive that she can feel a tiny pea through twenty mattresses and twenty feather beds, and she is convinced that the pea has given her a bruise. Many kids who worry are also supersensitive. They notice lots of things just like the princess did, like a scratchy tag in their clothes or a not-so-comfortable temperature in a room. They also tend to be really sensitive to uncomfortable feelings such as boredom or loneliness.

When kids who worry encounter these uncomfortable feelings, their tendency is to escape the situation. They take off the shirt with the uncomfortable tag or insist on leaving the restaurant that is too hot. They may try to fill their time with lots of activities to avoid feeling bored or always follow people around to escape feeling lonely. The problem is, their bodies get "out of practice" managing these feelings so their bodies feel even more uncomfortable than they would have if the kids hadn't avoided the feelings in the first place.

For You to Do

Let's help your body get some practice being "comfortable being uncomfortable" so you won't feel so lousy next time.

1.   Here is a list of feelings and situations that can make kids who worry feel uncomfortable and want to then escape or avoid. Choose three that you are particularly sensitive to.

_____   Staying in a room that is too hot or staying outside when it is too hot

_____   Staying in a room that is too cold or staying outside when it is too cold

_____   Doing nothing and being bored

_____   Being alone and feeling lonely

_____   Wearing a piece of clothing that is uncomfortable (because of an itchy tag, being too tight or too loose, a funny seam on a pair of socks, and so on)

_____   Feeling hungry

_____   Feeling thirsty

_____   Being in a situation that is too loud

_____   Being in a situation that is too crowded

2.   During the next week, be on alert for when these situations come up. As we've discussed, you will probably want to escape as quickly as possible. But instead, stick with it. On your first day, try to stay in the situation for at least five minutes. When that situation comes up again, add two minutes. When it comes up again, add another two minutes. Your goal is to be able to stay in these situations for at least ten minutes.

3.   Once you are able to stay in your uncomfortable situations for ten minutes or longer, let's give some thought as to why you are now able to stay when you used to run away. Check the ideas below if they apply to you:

_____   The longer I stayed, the easier it got.

_____   When I stayed in the situation, I figured out some strategies to make it easier for myself.

_____   When I stayed in the situation, I was able to focus on other things besides feeling uncomfortable.

_____   When I stayed in the situation, I actually had some fun.

_____   It was nice to see that I could cope.

_____   It is good to know I can do this, because this situation comes up for me a lot.

More to Do

When things cause us to worry, we tend to see a giant STOP sign in our brains. Very often, we STOP right in the middle of a scary situation and just EXIT. It's kind of like being on a highway. If we are scared or anxious, we find the nearest EXIT and get off the road. The problem with STOPPING and EXITING is that we never get to see what lies ahead or what happens next!

Let's practice doing something that will make you uncomfortable at first, but, with practice, will show you there is little to worry about. Could you plan two family movie nights? Depending on your age, you might need your parents' help selecting a movie (you only need one movie for this activity, even though it will stretch over two nights). Pick a movie that is scary but age appropriate. It should be a movie that you have not seen before. It must be a movie you can watch repeatedly in your home (rather than going to a movie theater). Ideally, you should not have heard about what happens at the end of the movie from your friends or siblings. It is perfectly fine to do this experiment with an episode of a TV show, too.

On the first night, turn the movie on. It is really important for you to pay attention to your thoughts and feelings and behaviors as you are watching. Notice when you start feeling really scared and nervous. Is your heart racing? Are your palms sweating? Are you covering your eyes or cowering behind a pillow? Are you feeling the urge to run out of the room?

When you notice these things, STOP and EXIT.

Yes, STOP the movie. And, EXIT family movie night.

At the moment you stop the movie, rate your anxiety from 0 to 10, with 0 being no anxiety and 10 being extremely anxious: _____

During the next day, write down any thoughts that pop into your mind about the movie and about your ability to cope with watching it:

_____

_____

_____

On the second night, restart your movie from the beginning. Again it is really important for you to pay attention to your thoughts and feelings and behaviors as you are watching. This time, however, you are going to see what happens next. Even if you feel anxious, you are going to keep watching…right until the very end.

At the end of the movie, rate your anxiety from 0 to 10, with 0 being no anxiety and 10 being extremely anxious: _____

Write down your thoughts about the movie and about your ability to cope with the movie now that you watched the entire thing:

_____

_____

_____

Often, when we stay in a fearful or uncertain situation, we learn that it was not that bad and that we could cope with it much better than we expected. In your life, as you did with the movie exercise, when you GO, rather than STOP and EXIT, you often see a happy ending and learn that you can cope with the scary thoughts and feelings along with way. Next time you are in a scary situation and feel like you want to STOP and EXIT, press the GO button in your brain instead. You might be pleasantly surprised by what you find!

Worry Can't Survive If You Are Flexible

For You to Know

People think they can control their worries by keeping things the same all the time. The problem with always trying to do things the same way is that life rarely lets that happen! Our world is full of change and uncertainty. So if you are too rigid with the rules you put in place, you are setting yourself up for failure.

You learned in earlier activities in this book that you can't control other people and situations. In this activity, you'll also learn that you can't control your worries. But you *can* learn to be flexible. When you are flexible, you are better able to handle changes in your routine.

Picture a pencil—it's really rigid, hard, not at all flexible. If you bend it, what happens? It cracks. Now imagine a piece of putty. If you bend it, no problem—it just makes a new shape. Nothing will break it, because it can adjust to any new form.

You are strongest when you are flexible. When you are flexible you can "bend" to adjust to any situation.

Let's get started teaching our brains to be more flexible.

For You to Do

Pick one thing that you do the same way all the time. If you can't think of anything, choose one thing that you always need to know about in advance. Here are some ideas:

- Eating the same lunch every day

- Always playing with the same friend after school

- Always having the same after-school pickup routine

- Needing to know what the plans are for the day ahead

Write down your habit: _____

_____

1. Get sticky notes or slips of paper and a pencil.

2. On each piece of paper, write a different choice you can make to change up your routine.

Example: *Harrison has taken a plain bagel, a green apple, and one Oreo for lunch every day for the past two years. He generated ideas for five different lunches he could try at school for a week:*

If your habit is always needing to know the plan for the day, your instruction is a little different. Instead, ask your parents to tell you several things that are planned for a Saturday or Sunday. Write each planned activity on a sticky note or strip of paper.

Example: *Helena has a strong need to know what's going to happen every day and in what order. Her mom gave her nine plans for Saturday, which Helena wrote on pieces of paper:*

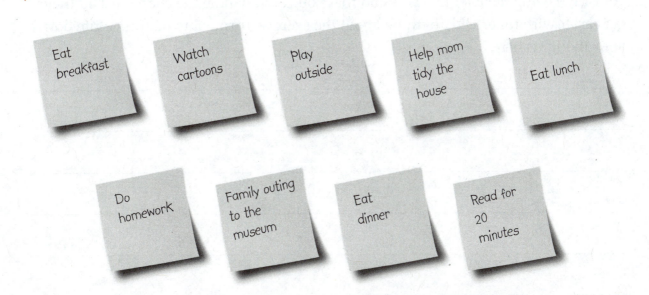

3.   Fold up your strips of paper and place them in a hat or a bowl. Each day for a week, select one slip each morning. That is your flexibility assignment for the day!

Example: *Harrison chose the slip of paper with "bagel with cream cheese, chocolate chip cookie, and apple" for his lunch on Monday. His dad helped him pack his lunch, and Harrison promised to try each item at lunchtime.*

If you are practicing being flexible within a single day, draw your first slip of paper out of your hat or bowl and do that activity. When you are done with that activity, select your next slip and do that activity, and so on. In other words, your day will take shape in whatever order you select your slips.

Example: *The first slip of paper Helena pulled out of a bowl was "Play outside." She wasn't used to playing outside so early in the morning, but she put on her jacket and had fun exploring. The next paper she chose read "Eat dinner." But it was only nine o'clock in the morning! She asked her parents if it was okay to have dinner for breakfast, and they thought it was a great idea. So she had pasta as her first meal.*

4.   Think about your experience of changing your routine. What did you learn from your time being flexible? Did you find that you could handle the changes? Did they get easier with time? Did anything about the exercise turn out to be fun? Write down your thoughts here:

_____

_____

_____

_____

_____

Being flexible takes practice. You should repeat the exercise you just did many times until it becomes easier. When you're comfortable with changes to your routine, challenge yourself to try the next step.

5.   Select a routine you want to challenge for this "Not Knowing" exercise. Then ask a parent to make a choice for you and not tell you. In other words, you are choosing to "not know" what's coming next. The goal is to show yourself that you can cope with "not knowing" and still have some fun!

Example: *For Harrison's "Not Knowing" exercise, he asked his dad to pack his lunch and not tell him what he packed. Harrison promised not to peek, and when it was lunchtime, he was pleasantly surprised! For Helena's "Not Knowing" exercise, she asked her mom to purposefully not tell her what they were doing Sunday afternoon. Although she was really worried when she got in the car, she was curious and excited to see what her mom was going to surprise her with.*

What did you learn from this Not Knowing challenge? Did you find that you could handle the surprise? Did anything about the exercise turn out to be fun? Write down your thoughts here:

_____

_____

_____

_____

_____

_____

More to Do

You have now learned how to be more flexible in your habits and routines. But did you know that your brain is just as flexible? In fact, you can teach your brain that even if things might be uncomfortable, new, or different, they are not dangerous.

Here is a list of practices that you can do to start retraining your brain to know that you're not in danger, that you're just doing something new, uncomfortable, or challenging. Make this list your own by adding in challenges that you regularly face.

Practice 1: Teach your brain that you're not in danger if you do something that you might not like or that you might find boring

- Read a book that you normally wouldn't pick up.

- Pick a new restaurant to go to that you aren't sure you'll like.

- _____

Practice 2: Teach your brain that you're not in danger if plans change

- Plan to go outside to play, but then have your parents change the plan.

- Plan a few things to do one evening when there definitely won't be enough time to do them all.

- _____

Practice 3: Teach your brain that you're not in danger if you're not good at something

- Play a game you've never played before.

- Draw a picture quickly and put it on your fridge or bedroom door.

- _____

Practice 4: Teach your brain that you're not in danger when things are not done in the way you always do them

- Sit in a chair you don't usually sit in for dinner.

- Sleep without the stuffed animal or blanket you normally sleep with (or sleep on the "other" side of your bed, or facing the other way).

- _____

Practice 5: Teach your brain that you're not in danger if you do something uncomfortable

- Wear a shirt that you don't like for at least two hours.

- Dress too warm on a hot day or too cool on a cold day.

- _____

These are just a few examples. Keep planning new and different flexibility practices using these lessons as a guide for what to keep working on. The more you do them, the more you'll notice that your brain will slow down and eventually stop sending so many worry thoughts.

Activity 20   Putting It All Together

For You to Know

Challenging our worries takes lots of baby steps. But gradually it can be done—in fact, *you've* done it! Practicing these steps in order, picking up the pace a bit, means that you can overcome your worries and fears more quickly—leaving less time for worries and more time for the things you enjoy.

The next time you notice your alarm going off; or you are feeling anxious, sad, or mad; or you think you might be caught in a Worry Cycle; follow these four steps:

1. **Spot the false alarm.** The situation is not dangerous—it's just new, difficult, and uncomfortable.

2. **Choose a useful thought.** Ask yourself, *Is what I am thinking accurate? Is what I am thinking useful?* If it seems like you are spending too much time thinking about these thoughts, then it's probably not useful. Ask yourself, *What is most likely to happen?* If it's a situation you've faced before, recall what actually happened. Figure out the most important things to focus on. Remember that the bad things we worry about don't usually happen. Remember that you've successfully handled other new, uncomfortable, or different situations before.

3. **Choose a different action.** Remember what you *can* control: your thoughts and your actions. Choose an action that will most likely lead to your end goal. Do the opposite of what the worry says. If the challenge seems too difficult, break it up into smaller pieces and practice one small step at a time.

4. **Keep practicing.** You may need to keep challenging your worry until your body can get used to a new habit or routine. The more you practice, the easier it gets. Your body will learn that the situation is not dangerous, and you won't have as many worries around it.

THe Worry Workbook for Kids

For You to Do

Let's practice using the steps here. This is Michael's Worry Cycle. Can you help him by completing the steps that he should take to break his Worry Cycle?

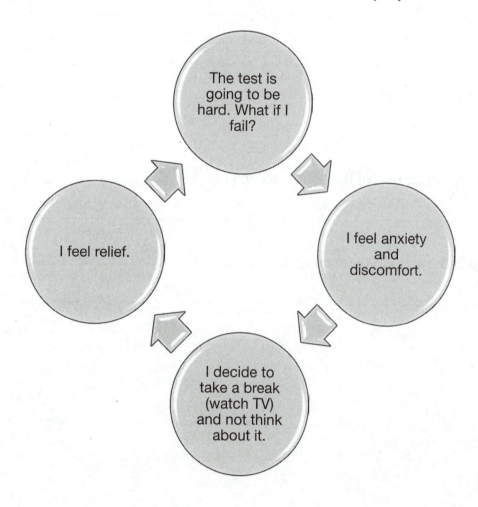

Michael's Worry Cycle

Is your alarm going off? Are you worrying, or feeling sad or mad?

Write down the worry: _____

_____

Challenge your worry: _____

_____

A more accurate or useful thought (choose your focus): _____

_____

Write down the action you choose: _____

_____

More to Do

We hope you'll use these steps whenever a worry or a new or uncomfortable situation arises. This week, use the steps to help feel ready to handle anything that comes up.

New or uncomfortable situation: _____

Is your alarm going off? Are you worrying, or feeling sad or mad?

Write down the worry: _____

_____

Challenge your worry: _____

_____

A more accurate or useful thought (choose your focus): _____

_____

Write down the action you choose: _____

_____

New or uncomfortable situation: _____

Is your alarm going off? Are you worrying, or feeling sad or mad?

Write down the worry: _____

_____

Challenge your worry: _____

_____

A more accurate or useful thought (choose your focus): _____

_____

Write down the action you choose: _____

The action you choose: _____

_____

Congratulations!

You have learned how to identify your worry, challenge anxious thoughts, and plan for and practice doing things that are new or uncomfortable. The more you practice challenging anxious thoughts, staying focused on what is really important, and doing more things that you used to avoid, the less your alarm will go off because you now have:

- Proof against anxious thoughts

- Evidence that you can manage or cope in difficult situations

- Trained your body to know that it's not dangerous, that you just have to "get used to it"

Habits that Help

Ten-Minute Mindfulness

For You to Know

You may have heard about *mindfulness* at school or in a book. "Mindfulness" is a word that means paying attention to the things happening in and around you right now. Being mindful, or focusing on the present moment, also means not judging what is happening around you or reacting to it. It means being just an observer.

In activity 10, Choose Your Focus, you learned that almost all worries are usually about either the past or the future. And, because you can't change the past or control the future, you learned that the best thing to do is be aware of where you are and what you're doing *right now*.

Paying attention to the present moment can be difficult. It takes a lot of practice. But being mindful is a skill that can break the Worry Cycle, especially when you approach the situation with care and kindness.

For You to Do

Try to fit in this ten-minute mindfulness practice every day. Plan a time that will work best: maybe first thing in the morning, right after school, or before you get ready for bed. Try different times to see which fits best on a daily basis. Even after just a few days of practicing, you'll notice that you're better at getting focused and that your worries aren't taking up all of your time. Follow these steps:

1. Find a comfortable seat and sit in a comfortable position.

2. Take a slow, steady, deep breath. Feel the air fill up your lungs, then slowly let it out.

3. Keep taking slow and steady deep breaths. Feel the air fill you up, then slowly let it out.

4. Now try to pay attention to this moment *right now*. Don't think about whether this moment is good or bad. Keep your mind open, without judgment. You might concentrate on your senses: What is the quietest sound you can hear? What are all the things you can smell? How does the air feel around you? How does the chair feel that you are sitting on?

5. Observe and notice, without judgment, for a few minutes.

6. End with a few slow, steady, deep breaths.

Doing a ten-minute mindfulness practice daily will help you have fewer false alarms. And it will help you get back to the present more quickly—so that you aren't getting stuck worrying about the past or the future.

More to Do

You might notice that whenever you are worrying or nervous, your parents or others might tell you to "relax" or "calm down."

But it's hard to calm down when your mind is racing with worries and your alarm is going off. And like we discussed in activity 5, Let It Come and Go, it's even harder if you and everyone around you is trying to "make it go away."

Here is a simple breathing and muscle-relaxation exercise that you can do each day to help you stay more relaxed if your body is feeling tense or your alarm is going off too often:

1. First, take a slow deep breath for a count of 5. Take the full count, starting to inhale at 1 and ending at 5. Count silently to yourself: 1–2–3–4–5. Then let it out for a count of 5: 1–2–3–4–5.

2. Breathe in again, through your nose, 1–2–3–4–5. Then breathe out through your mouth, 1–2–3–4–5. Again, take a deep breath, making sure you fill up your belly, 1–2–3–4–5. Now let it out, 1–2–3–4–5. Again, inhale, 1–2–3–4–5, and exhale, 1–2–3–4–5.

3. Close your eyes and feel your body beginning to relax.

4. Now, ball up your right hand into a fist. Squeeze for a count of 5, then relax your hand for a count of 5. One more time, squeeze, 1–2–3–4–5. Then relax, 1–2–3–4–5. Squeeze again, 1–2–3–4–5, and let go, 1–2–3–4–5.

5. Now, ball up your left hand into a fist. Squeeze for a count of 5, then relax your hand for a count of 5. One more time, squeeze, 1–2–3–4–5. Then relax, 1–2–3–4–5. Squeeze again, 1–2–3–4–5, and let go, 1–2–3–4–5.

You may be feeling more relaxed now. You can squeeze and relax other muscles in your body such as your stomach, thighs, even your toes! Stay focused on the count and on the movement of the muscle.

By breathing slow and steady, and relaxing your muscles, you're teaching your body that there's no danger and that it's okay to "calm down."

Take an Insta-Break

For You to Know

Most kids today report that they relax most often by checking their phone, going on their computer, or watching TV. These are acceptable ways to relax *sometimes*. But if you're doing them *all the time*, you might be feeling more tired and anxious than you'd expect.

We live in a really busy world. Between school, activities, friends, family, and technology, our brains and bodies stay active for hours each day. Everyone needs a break from time to time. We especially need to take a brain and body break when we are nervous or anxious. It turns out that visiting social media sites and watching shows aren't the best ways to relax—in fact, they can add a lot of stress to your life.

Going on devices to watch videos, movies, or check social media posts might make you feel like you should be more attractive, funnier, smarter, more talented, more popular. You can end up feeling not good enough or feeling sad when you don't have what others have. Although these feelings aren't exactly a Worry Cycle, they work the same way. Instead of relaxing during your free time, you end up feeling exhausted and bad.

For You to Do

There are a lot of ways to relax that really do bring pleasure. Next time you need to find your calm, use this worksheet to remind you of what you can do to take a break. In the chart below, list your favorite Take a Break activities. We've included a few ideas to get you started.

Take a Break

Nature	Look for pretty leaves or flowers in your yard or at the park	Water plants, pull out weeds, or plant new bulbs	Go for a hike
Education	Read a book (something silly or serious)	Research a topic you find interesting	Write in your journal
Sports	Take a walk (maybe with a dog?)	Go for a swim	Ride a bike
Art	Take pictures or make a video just for yourself	Paint or draw	Work on a scrapbook or create an inspiration board
Projects	Do an errand or chore that's been on your to-do list	Decorate your room	Organize your closet or desk
Other (fill in your own ideas)			

More to Do

Another technique that encourages taking a break is called *visualization*. Here are steps to a visualization exercise that can give your brain and body a time-out.

1. Set aside at least ten minutes when you will not be interrupted and when you do not need to go and do anything (like leaving for school).

2. Find a quiet, comfy place to sit or lie down.

3. Close your eyes and imagine that you are in a submarine submerged in a calm, peaceful ocean. Imagine sitting in a comfy seat in that submarine and watching the sea float by outside the window. Maybe you'll see some brightly colored coral. Some beautiful fish floating by in a school. A bit of seaweed bobbing along.

4. For ten minutes, all you need to do is *see*. Just watch this calming scene in your imagination. Lie still to give your body a break. If your mind drifts to worries or other thoughts, bring it back to the ocean. If you get distracted by the sounds around you, just tune in to your own breath. If your house is really noisy, try putting some big, padded earphones on next time you try this exercise.

If you aren't into the ocean, you can try this exercise in outer space. Imagine that you are tethered to your rocket ship. You're outfitted in a cool space suit and a glass-fronted helmet. In outer space, there is no noise. All you can hear is the sound of your own breath. What do you see go by? Do you see the stars twinkling? Can you look down at Earth? How about up at the moon and the other planets in the solar system? Remember to lie still to give your body a break. If your mind drifts to worries or other thoughts, bring it back to outer space.

Sleep Solutions

For You to Know

Isn't it funny that as soon as we get into bed at night, our brains wake up? All of a sudden, we are thinking of a million things we have to do and another million things that might go wrong the next day. There are two problems here. First, nighttime is a really bad time to get things done. Second, worry gets in the way of sleep.

Colin was losing out on a lot of sleep worrying about the overnight fifth-grade field trip to an outdoor recreation center. This trip, which so many kids looked forward to at the end of elementary school, was not sounding terribly exciting to Colin. He was fine all day when he was busy with school and activities and his friends. But as soon as he got into bed at night, it was as if his brain switched to "Field Trip TV."

Colin was worrying about *everything*. Who would he be assigned to share a room with? What if that person wasn't a close friend? What if he missed his parents? What if he didn't like the food? He had no idea what activities they would be doing all day, and not knowing made him very nervous too. When he took trips with his family, his parents made sure he knew every detail of the itinerary in advance. Colin also didn't want to admit to any of his friends that he had a lot of fears. What if it thundered on the field trip? What if it was too dark in the room? What if they had to swim in a lake that contained fish or other scary creatures? The list went on and on, keeping him up into the wee hours of the morning for weeks before the trip.

For You to Do

As we already mentioned, there are two problems when your brain switches over to the worry channel at night. First, you have no way of addressing your questions at night. Neither did Colin. He realized that even if he found out some answers in the morning, he came up with new worries that night. Second, worry really interferes with sleep. Interestingly, Colin found that as he got more tired, his worries felt more real and he felt less able to fight back. You might have noticed this pattern with sleep and anxiety in your own life too.

Thankfully, there are helpful strategies you can use at night—and none of them involve bringing your worries to bed! The things we talked about in Activity 22 can be of great help at night. Visualization and other insta-breaks can work wonders at bedtime, so long as they are calm and quiet (for example, reading, drawing, writing in a journal, cuddling with the family dog, having a long bath). Another good strategy to try is incorporating Worry Boxes into your nighttime routine.

Worry Boxes

1.   Find three shoe boxes or plastic boxes. If you are creative, this is your time to shine. Decorate your boxes any way you like, and label your boxes as shown below. If you aren't into creative stuff, you can just label your boxes.

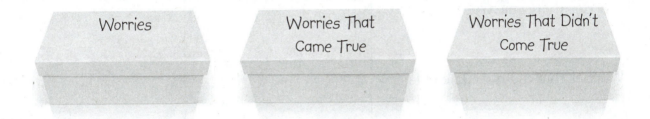

Worries | Worries That Came True | Worries That Didn't Come True

2.   Place a stack of sticky notes or slips of paper and a pen next to your worry boxes.

3.   Each night, write down your worries. One worry per slip of paper. Make your worries really specific. For example, rather than writing, "I will do badly on my spelling test," write, "I will get all ten words wrong on my spelling test."

4.   Put the worries in your Worries box. When you put your worries in the Worries box, it is as if you are removing those worries from your brain for the night. These worries require no further thought. It is now time for bed. Good night!

5.   The next day, sort your worries. Take a worry from the Worries box and place it into either the Worries That Came True box or the Worries That Didn't Come True box. Sometimes, you might have to leave a worry in your Worries box because you don't yet know the outcome. For example, if you haven't got your spelling test back yet, you can leave that worry in your Worries box until you get your grade.

6.   Keep doing this activity every night for two or three weeks.

More to Do

After two or three weeks (or if any of your boxes begin to overflow!), it is time to do a tally. Go ahead and count all of the worries in your boxes.

	Number of worries
Worries that came true	
Worries that did not come true	

What do you notice from your worry tally? Did most of your worries come true or not come true?

_____

_____

_____

Did any of your worries get placed in the Worries box five times or more? If so, which worries?

_____

_____

_____

Do those worries always end up with the same outcome? Yes   No

Most kids find that they have the same worries over and over again, and that the outcome for those repetitive worries is always the same—*not true*!

What this means is that you don't have to keep your Worry Boxes forever. Once you see some patterns, you can "short-circuit" your worries with simple brain boss backs. You can say to yourself:

Hey brain, you're telling me lies.

Not going to happen.

I've heard that one before.

Can you think of any boss backs that work well for your worries?

_____

_____

_____

Who's the Judge of Me?

For You to Know

When you were a really little kid—like three or four—did you ever wear crazy outfits that didn't match? Go to preschool without brushing your hair? Just start dancing in line at the bank with your mom or singing loudly in a restaurant? Kids of this age are so awesome because they really don't care much what people think of them.

As we grow up, we become more and more aware of how people see us. Sometimes this can be a good thing. When you bring home a beautiful painting or a great grade on a test, it is nice to see your parents looking really happy. A piano teacher might complement you on playing a piece with a lot of emotion. Or a friend might write something really special about you on your birthday card. Knowing that someone sees you in a good light feels good, doesn't it?

Unfortunately, there are also judgmental people out there in the world. And judgmental people are really difficult to please. You might have a really critical coach who never says a kind word. Or a person who says she is your friend but teases your clothes or refuses to sit with you at lunch.

The tricky thing about judgmental people is that as hard as we try to impress them, they might still not be satisfied. In these cases, you can do a bit of judging too! It is okay to decide that you don't want to try so hard anymore. Maybe there are some people who you just don't want to have as a big part of your life. The best coaches are the ones who teach with kindness and encouragement. And the best friends are those who love us for who we truly are, even if we aren't in the popular crowd, if we wear a silly shirt, or if we do something embarrassing.

Keep in mind this great quotation from Bernard Baruch, who was an advisor to two presidents nearly one hundred years ago: "Be who you are and say what you feel, because those who mind don't matter and those who matter don't mind."

For You to Do

Take a moment and write down the five people you care about the most in the world:

1. _____

2. _____

3. _____

4. _____

5. _____

Now, think back over the past week or two. Think about times when you had thoughts like:

I bet he thinks I'm a loser.

I wonder if she thinks my shirt is ugly.

If I mess up in front of those kids, I'd be so embarrassed.

When you had thoughts like this—thoughts of people judging you—who were you thinking about? Take a moment and write down the names of five people who you worried were judging you in a negative way recently.

1. _____

2. _____

3. _____

4. _____

5. _____

Did the names of the people you care about the most in your life match up with the names of the people who you worried were judging you in the past week?

More to Do

Most people care what other people think of them. This is human nature! Kids and teens tend to worry about what others think of them even more than adults. We tend to forget to take a step back and ask ourselves:

What do I think about this person who might be judging me?

Is this someone who I care deeply about?

Is this someone who I value as a friend?

How do you feel about the people who you worried might be judging you during the past week? Do you think very positively about them, or do you feel quite negatively about them? Maybe something in the middle? Write down your thoughts:

_____

_____

_____

_____

_____

_____

Sprinkle in Some Fun

For You to Know

When you spend time doing things you enjoy, it's harder to stay worried. Even difficult tasks or chores seem easier to handle when you're fitting in fun activities. Be sure to schedule in things you like to do—that way you still take care of all of those things you *have* to do while not missing out on anything fun.

Maybe you have a lot of projects and tests at school this week. Or you have a lot of sports and lessons after school, so you won't be home until late all month. You may be thinking about all of the things you *have* to do, and you may be worried that you won't be able to do the things you actually *want* to do. You might be telling yourself, *I'll never get it all done* or *I won't have any time to relax.* This may cause you to start feeling stressed and overwhelmed. It's time to take a step back, look at what you have to do, plan when you'll do it, and be sure to "sprinkle" in some fun.

You now know how to ignore the false alarms and remember to stay focused on the "big picture." Keep in mind that that big picture also includes the fun things in life. So this week, make a plan to sprinkle in the good stuff. You may be surprised to find that you'll have time to get everything done that you have to *and* also have enough time to have some fun.

For You to Do

To get started with your planning, let's first brainstorm the things you want to include.

1.   List some activities you'd like to make sure you have time for this week that are fun and enjoyable.

_____

_____

_____

_____

2.   List the things that are already scheduled, like school, afterschool activities, appointments, and so on.

_____

_____

_____

_____

3.   Then list the things that you really need to finish this week (which might not be fun).

_____

_____

_____

_____

Now put everything on your lists into your new weekly calendar:

Weekly Planner

Schedule for _____ – _____

	Monday	Tuesday	Wednesday	Thursday	Friday	Saturday	Sunday
8–2pm							
3pm							
4pm							
5pm							
6pm							
7pm							
8pm							
9pm							

Helping Children to Overcome Anxiety and the Fear of Uncertainty

Sprinkle in Some Fun

Making a plan that has fun sprinkled in makes it easier to stick to. It also makes it easier to see how you'll get everything done so you won't feel overwhelmed. If you need more Weekly Planner sheets, photocopy the blank one near the end of this book.

Appendix

Extra Worksheets

The following worksheets are also available for download at http://www.newharbinger.com/39638. For more tips for parents, don't forget to visit http://www.worrywisekids.org.

My Worry Cycle

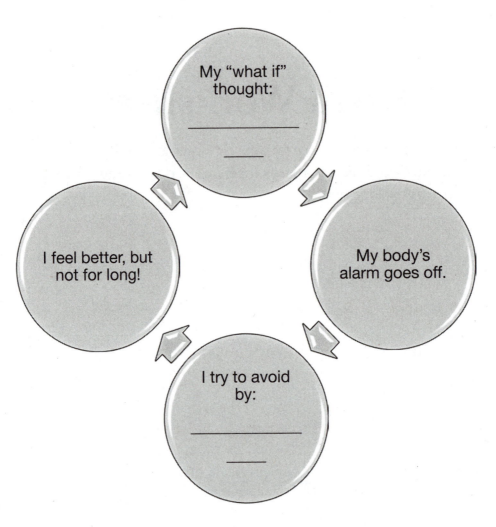

My Worry Cycle

Challenging Worry Worksheet

Situation	Worry or Anxious Thought	Feeling	Challenge the Worry (think of a more accurate and useful thought)

Practice Ladder

Worry about _____

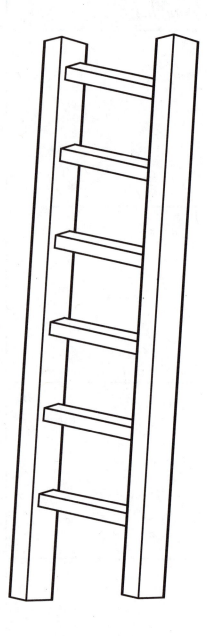

The Worry Workbook for Kids

Weekly Planner

Schedule for _____ – _____

	Monday	Tuesday	Wednesday	Thursday	Friday	Saturday	Sunday
8–2pm							
3pm							
4pm							
5pm							
6pm							
7pm							
8pm							
9pm							

Helping Children to Overcome Anxiety and the Fear of Uncertainty

Acknowledgments

This workbook could not have been written if not for the decades of research and important work done by the dedicated researchers and clinicians in the field of childhood anxiety.

We would like to specifically acknowledge the work of Dr. Philip C. Kendall, whose Coping Cat (Kendall and Hedtke 2006) treatment and writings on childhood anxiety have provided the clinical foundation and evidence base for the cognitive-behavioral principles on which the activities in this workbook are based. The activities were also shaped by the writings and teachings of the outstanding researchers, clinicians, and mentors Dr. John Piacentini, Dr. Anne Marie Albano, Dr. Martin Franklin, Dr. John March, and Dr. Tamar Chansky. Collectively, we thank you all, and those whom we may have inadvertently missed. Our confidence in the techniques we have shared rests on your invaluable contributions.

We would like to thank our colleagues at the Children and Adult's Center for OCD and Anxiety—Drs. Tamar Chansky, Lynne Siqueland, Chiara Baxt, and Larina Kase—for their infinite support, collaboration, and, especially, their thoughtful understanding of anxious youth.

Finally, we would like to acknowledge all of the children and their parents who have worked with us and gave us the opportunity to participate in their lives, and for teaching and inspiring us every day.

Reference

Kendall, P. C., and K. A. Hedtke. 2006. *Cognitive-Behavioral Therapy for Anxious Children: Therapist Manual*, third edition. Ardmore, PA: Workbook Publishing.

The Worry Workbook for Kids

Recommended Reading

Albano, A. M., with L. Pepper. 2013 *You and Your Anxious Child: Free Your Child from Fears and Worries and Create a Joyful Family Life*. New York: Avery/Penguin Press.

Chansky, T. E. 2014. *Freeing Your Child from Anxiety: Practical Strategies to Overcome Fears, Worries, and Phobias and Be Prepared for Life—From Toddlers to Teens*. Second edition. New York: Harmony Books/Random House.

Rapee, R., S. Spence, V. Cobham, and A. Wignall. 2008. *Helping Your Anxious Child: A Step-by-Step Guide for Parents*. Oakland, CA: New Harbinger Publications.

For more tips for parents, don't forget to visit: http://www.worrywisekids.com.

Muniya S. Khanna, PhD, is a clinical psychologist at the Children's and Adult Center for OCD and Anxiety, director of The OCD and Anxiety Institute, and research investigator at the Children's Hospital of Philadelphia. Prior to this, she served on the faculty of the University of Pennsylvania School of Medicine. She is an expert in the cognitive-behavioral treatment of childhood anxiety and obsessive-compulsive spectrum disorders, having been involved in some of the most important research in the field in the last twenty years. Khanna is author of numerous scientific papers, chapters, and treatment manuals, and a recognized cognitive behavioral therapy (CBT) trainer and speaker. She is a pioneer in digital mental health research for child anxiety. In partnership with her mentor, Philip Kendall, she developed digital interventions for child anxiety, including Camp Cope-A-Lot, Child Anxiety Tales; and hostswww.copingcatparents.com, a website to inform and empower parents of children with anxiety.

Deborah Roth Ledley, PhD, is a licensed clinical psychologist at the Children's and Adult Center for OCD and Anxiety. Ledley received her PhD in psychology from the University of Toronto in 1999, and completed a postdoctoral fellowship at the Adult Anxiety Clinic of Temple at Temple University. She then spent several years on faculty at the University of Pennsylvania at the Center for the Treatment and Study of Anxiety. Since 2006, Ledley has been in private practice in the suburbs of Philadelphia, PA, where she primarily works with children, adolescents, and adults with anxiety disorders. She has published over fifty scientific papers and book chapters, as well as four academic books, including *Making Cognitive-Behavioral Therapy Work* and *Becoming a Calm Mom*. Ledley has been quoted in magazines such as *Parents*, *Fit Pregnancy*, *Family Fun*, and *Countdown*, as well as on several websites, including www.forbes.com, www.cnn.com, and www.iparentinglife.com.

Foreword writer **Tamar Chansky, PhD,** is a psychologist and author of several popular books, including *Freeing Your Child from Negative Thinking*, *Freeing Your Child from Anxiety*, and *Freeing Your Child from Obsessive-Compulsive Disorder*. Chansky is passionate about helping kids, parents, and other adults pursue the lives they want to lead, free from the obstacles of anxiety, pessimism, and obsessive-compulsive disorder (OCD). Visit her website at www.tamarchansky.com.

MORE BOOKS *from*
NEW HARBINGER PUBLICATIONS

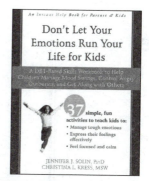

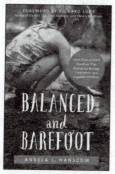
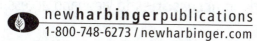

Register your **new harbinger** titles for additional benefits!

When you register your **new harbinger** title—purchased in any format, from any source—you get access to benefits like the following:

- Downloadable accessories like printable worksheets and extra content

- Instructional videos and audio files

- Information about updates, corrections, and new editions

Not every title has accessories, but we're adding new material all the time.

Access free accessories in 3 easy steps:

1. Sign in at NewHarbinger.com (or **register** to create an account).

2. Click on **register a book**. Search for your title and click the **register** button when it appears.

3. Click on the **book cover or title** to go to its details page. Click on **accessories** to view and access files.

That's all there is to it!

If you need help, visit:

NewHarbinger.com/accessories

new harbinger
CELEBRATING
40 YEARS